FOUR YEARS WITH THE DEMON RUM 1925-1929

The autobiography and diary of temperance inspector Clifford Rose

Edited with an introduction by E.R. Forbes and A.A. MacKenzie

ACADIENSIS PRESS

FIRST EDITION
PUBLISHED BY:

ACADIENSIS PRESS
CAMPUS HOUSE
University of New Brunswick
P.O. Box 4400
Fredericton, New Brunswick
E3B   5A3   (506)   453-4978

HV
5091
.C2
R67

ISBN   0-919107-00-1

SOURCES IN THE HISTORY OF
ATLANTIC CANADA No. 1

GENERAL EDITORS: P.A. BUCKNER AND
E.R. FORBES

Typeset and Printed by Keystone Printing & Lithographing Ltd., Saint John, N.B.

TABLE OF CONTENTS

INTRODUCTION

The prohibition crusade in Nova Scotia was an integral part of a general movement for progressive reform which swept across North America at the turn of the century.[1] Stimulated by accelerating technical progress and jolted by the intensifying social problems created by industrialization, many North Americans were convinced of the need and feasibility of reform. Concerned with such problems as poverty, disease, human exploitation, the excessive power of corporations, and partisanship and corruption in politics, they placed their faith in governments and legislation as the agents of reform.[2] Their reform blueprints were frequently optimistic in the extreme. Henry George, whose ideas were popular among Canadian labour, found a panacea in a single tax on land.[3] Edward Bellamy envisioned a reconstruction of society upon rational lines to protect the weak from exploitation and redistribute a share of the national wealth to all. In Nova Scotia, A.P. Reid, a medical doctor and director of the Halifax insane asylum, outlined a programme which included a government-sponsored social security scheme and massive government intervention in the economy to mitigate booms and slumps. These measures, he assured his listeners, "would revolutionize society, by enthroning comfort and independence on the cold and heartless pinnacles of crime, dissipation, poverty and misery that overshadowed every civilized land. Darkness will give way to light, and the sombre become diffused with joy".[4]

Millenarian visions were also expressed in religious terms. As the clergy became more socially aware, they searched the scriptures for explanations and remedies for their communities' problems and often found the answer in a more collective approach to salvation. Christ, they discovered, had been concerned not only with the individual but with society: he was "the greatest social reformer the world has ever seen".[5] He had left a potential design for reform in such teachings as the sermon on the mount, the Lord's Prayer and the golden rule. An ideal community, the Kingdom of God, could be realized on earth if Christ's followers restructured society according to his teachings. The Social Gospel, as the new creed became known, fired the imaginations of a generation of young, idealistic Protestant clergy and thrust them into the van of the many progressive crusades which proliferated in the early decades of the twentieth century.[6] Roman Catholics too evolved a Social Catholicism which often justified their involvement in these movements.[7]

Within the general campaign to restructure society, goals and emphases, often reflecting differing occupational interests, varied widely. Trade unions grew in strength and their leaders lobbied governments, and vi

entered politics directly, sometimes with the ultimate goal of creating a socialist state.[8] Women lobbied governments for health and welfare legislation and sought the franchise as the key to their own emancipation.[9] Farmers organized cooperatives and entered politics as an occupational group.[10] Even entrepreneurs, while resisting reforms which seemed to threaten their interests, enthusiastically endorsed those which promised them more efficient government services.[11] Support for prohibition came from all of these groups. Middle class reformers believed the consumption of alcohol to be involved in practically every social issue with which they were concerned. They saw it as a causal factor in poverty, crime, disease, industrial and automobile accidents, abuse of women and children, and even the subversion of the electoral process.[12] Businessmen found alcohol a barrier to their goal of a more disciplined labour force, while J.B. McLachlan, union leader and radical socialist, proclaimed it a weapon of the corporations in undermining the solidarity and effectiveness of unions.[13] To farmers the growing consumption of alcohol seemed a part of the general threat to their values and way of life resulting from industrialization and the growth of cities.[14] Prohibition thus drew support from both progressive and conservative elements in Canadian society.

Nova Scotia had a strong temperance tradition dating from the early nineteenth century. While various temperance organizations, including the Sons of Temperance, the Women's Christian Temperance Union, and the temperance societies of the evangelical churches did not secure prohibition, they did make drinking less respectable, closing taverns and eliminating rum in the payment of wages. They also succeeded in driving alcohol from the parlour to the woodshed in many Canadian homes.[15] At the turn of the century the progressives brought new allies, a more formidable leadership and a more attractive justification to an already impressive organization for the war on booze.

In 1904 H.R. Grant, a Presbyterian clergyman, left his congregation at Stellarton, Pictou County, for full-time temperance activity. Chairman of the Temperance Committee of the Maritime Synod of the Presbyterian Church, Grant used the Committee as a forum for interjecting the ideas of the social gospel into the debates of the regional Synod and ultimately secured its support for prohibition.[16] In 1907 Grant became secretary of the provincial section of the Dominion Alliance which co-ordinated activities of the various temperance organizations in the province. Ten years later he accepted the office of secretary of the Social Service Council of Nova Scotia, established in 1909 as a co-operative effort by the various Protestant denominations to hasten the coming of the "Kingdom".

Nonetheless, despite the power of the groups which Grant represented, progress came slowly. Governments were still aware of the prohibition experiment in New Brunswick half a century before when the anger of those barred from their favourite beverage proved stronger than the gratitude of the temperance forces.[17] The Liberals, in power in Nova Scotia after 1882, made gestures in support of prohibition which stopped short of preventing anyone who really wanted liquor from obtaining it. The division of responsibilities between federal and provincial authorities facilitated an ambiguous policy. Only the federal government could prevent the manufacture of alcoholic beverages within the country and their transport across national or provincial boundaries. Only a provincial government could bar their sale and transport within a province. Stalled at the federal level after Laurier declared the results of the 1898 plebiscite inconclusive, prohibitionists focussed their efforts on the provinces.[18] In Nova Scotia, they drafted the bills they wanted introduced, offered their backing to candidates pledged to support prohibition, and mounted a steadily growing campaign of agitation and propaganda. In 1910 the government bowed to their pressure, passing a bill to bar the sale and transport of booze within the province outside of Halifax. By 1914 the prohibitionists were within one vote of the majority they needed to extend provincial prohibition to that city.[19]

The advent of war added a new urgency to the progressives' call for discipline and efficiency. Provincial prohibition came into force in all provinces by the end of 1917 and early in the following year the federal government completed the process by barring importation and manufacture. The War also strengthened the progressives' faith that the new society which they envisioned was imminent and would emerge from the reconstruction which would follow the War.[20] This optimism was reflected in Nova Scotia at the War's end in bursts of trade union and co-operative activity, forays by farmers and labour into provincial politics and, with women voting for the first time, the overwhelming endorsement of prohibition in the plebiscite of 1920. However, the expectations of the reformers were universally doomed to disappointment. The corporations successfully isolated and smashed experiments with industrial unionism in Amherst in the summer of 1919. An economic recession which began the following summer revealed serious structural weaknesses in the Maritime economy and ushered in a crushing regional depression. Unions collapsed amid massive unemployment and those that remained struggled to retain the gains already achieved.[21] The farmer and labour political movements, after a significant showing in the 1920 provincial election, quickly disintegrated. Maritimers turned to parties which had some chance of gaining power nationally and therefore offered hope of alleviating the region's urgent economic and social problems. The provincial government indefinitely postponed such progressive measures as widow's pensions and the minimum wage and deflected other demands for reform with the plea that implementation would have to await financial "justice" from the federal government.[22] Journalists and boards of trade led a campaign for the redress of Maritime economic grievances behind the slogan "Maritime Rights", but this movement also tended to raise hopes which, after the Maritimers had been diverted by a series of royal commissions, were ultimately disappointed.[23]

Prohibition too could not escape the general disillusionment. It did not yield any dramatic decrease in crime, disease or poverty. Newspaper reports of rum-running, bootlegging and even gang warfare in the underworld (the last taken exclusively from the American press) suggested that prohibition was at best a mixed blessing. Prohibitionists claimed that prohibition had not been given a fair test since the government had not seriously tried to enforce it. When the Conservatives under E.N. Rhodes came to power in 1925 they promised a sincere effort at enforcement and appointed D.K. Grant (no relation to H.R. Grant), clergyman, lawyer and prohibitionist, as chief inspector in charge of policing the temperance legislation in the province. His changes in the enforcement bureaucracy led indirectly to the vacancy which brought Clifford Rose into the front lines of the war against demon rum.[24]

Rose's autobiography and diary suggest an optimism and subsequent disillusionment which was not untypical of the period. A self-educated carpenter, Rose was drawn to an interest in social problems through a church brotherhood, itself a product of the social gospel. But he found the church's blueprints and tactics for achieving reform less plausible than those offered by the veteran labour leaders whom he met in the trade union councils. His progressive enthusiasm found expression in the labour movement which he served as president of the local carpenters' union, secretary of the Pictou County Trades and Labour Council and as an active campaigner in labour's foray into provincial politics in the election of 1920.[25] The collapse of this movement in defeat and recrimination brought bitter disillusionment. As Rose later wrote at the age of thirty-six, life had "passed its zenith leaving shattered illusions, shattered opinions and shattered idols".[26] The depression of the early 1920s forced Rose to consider his own urgent financial needs. Hoping to barter his services as a political campaigner for a government job, Rose worked for the Conservatives in the provincial election of 1925. But others had the same idea and the government could not begin to meet the claims of its supporters for jobs and patronage. Rose ultimately received the reward for his labours in municipal politics. With his party controlling the New Glasgow town council, Rose was appointed municipal temperance inspector when the incumbent, Tom McKay, accepted an appointment as a provincial inspector. The whole structure of prohibition enforcement was at this time a complicated network of overlapping jurisdictions. D.K. Grant presided over a corps of provincial inspectors, each of whom was responsible for a section of territory usually covering two or more counties. Towns and municipalities might employ one or more temperance inspectors or constables to enforce prohibition within their bailwicks. The federal government employed a corps of preventive officers to combat smuggling and revenue officers to ferret out stills, and both groups were assisted after 1920 by a small force of Royal Canadian Mounted Police.[27] Working unofficially to keep all these on their toes were the prohibitionists themselves led by the redoubtable H.R. Grant. Those who supplied the booze had worked out a more efficient division of labour. Fishermen and shipowners who had developed expertise in supplying thirsty Americans with rum from the West Indies and brandy and whiskey from St. Pierre and Miquelon — a practice tolerated by Canadian authorities — extended their operations to the illegal supply of the home market. They sold liquor "over the side" of their vessels to gangs of smugglers who carried it in motor cars to the bootleggers who passed it on, often in a well-watered condition, to the consumers.

Despite their number and variety the enforcement officers did not curtail the liquor traffic in the province. After less than a week in office Clifford Rose reported the rum dives in New Glasgow to be "thick as bees" and testified that not only was New Glasgow "rotten to the core" but his position as temperance inspector was "rotten" as well.[28] His job, Rose discovered, was far from a straightforward battle against the liquor trade. Members of his party aimed to wrest control of the illegal trade from the Liberals and secure it for themselves. Liberals were fair game for arrest; Conservatives were not only to be left alone, but even protected from "rival" officers. Another of his duties was to secure revenue for the town council — a matter of some importance in a community hard-hit by depression. In one year, for example, Rose could boast that he had brought $10,000 in fines into municipal coffers. As an incentive, enforcement officers frequently received a percentage of the fines from convictions obtained. In New Glasgow the Council expressed appreciation for Rose's efforts through frequent increases in salary. These rewards were intended to encourage zeal on the part of the police, but they were actually a deterrent since no one wished to kill the goose that laid the golden eggs. The officers and the municipalities could only expect maximum revenues while the trade was flourishing. Heavy jail sentences, property confiscations or excessive harrassment were bad business for all concerned. An occasional raid, a moderate fine, a temporary shutdown usually served to placate the vigilant "drys" without seriously interrupting the lucrative flow of spirits. Rose became increasingly cynical as he accommodated himself to his new job. A system in which money and political advantage were primary motivations left little room for any reform idealism which Rose still possessed. Indeed, when the government party ordered the inspector out of town for an election so that his presence would not inhibit the illegal activities of its workers, what moral basis was there for attacking rum-runners and bootleggers? Rose concluded that there was none. It was merely a game in which the rum-runners and enforcement officers operated on a common plane. Each had found a means of economic survival in a period of hard times. For Rose his new employment brought liberation from the economic bondage which condemned the working class to a cheerless existence. For the first time he had the opportunity to appreciate the rich life which his province afforded to those who had the time and money to enjoy it. There was a strong note of exhilaration in his description of his fishing trips, the first for him in many years, the beauties of local scenery of which rides in his new automobile made him suddenly conscious, and the enjoyment of summers with his family at his new cottage near Pictou Landing. These had been made possible by the demon rum to which Rose was duly grateful.

Though willing to work toward the goals of his party and the munici-pality which employed him, Rose found his position a precarious one. As word of the proliferation of the rum dives in New Glasgow reached Halifax, Chief D.K. Grant and his inspectors swooped down on Rose's territory in a series of raids whose success could have exposed Rose's toler-ation of the forces of evil. Tipped off by a friend, however, Rose made a series of raids on suspected premises which he had been "saving" for just such an eventuality. He then upstaged the outsiders by securing convic-tions while they were unable to do so. But the prohibitionists became restive as the booze trade continued to flourish in their community. A local clergyman berated Rose from the pulpit, a newly elected Liberal alderman attacked him in the council and James A. Fraser, the ancient but peppery editor of the Liberal *Eastern Chronicle*, jeered at him in the press.[29] Nevertheless these problems were less serious than that which arose from a falling out of Conservative notables, Fred Milligan and Walter Weir, in a squabble over town lots. Since Rose was a Milligan supporter and Tom McKay, the provincial inspector for the district, was Weir's partner in real estate investment, they were drawn into the feud, aggravating personal relations already strained in a previous rivalry over fines. As McKay moved against Milligan's protégés in the trade, Rose arrested his own friends to prevent McKay from receiving the credit. So intolerable had Rose's position become that in 1929, when prohibition was again tested in a provincial plebiscite, Rose rejoiced at its defeat. Prohibition was then replaced with so-called "government control", a government monopoly of the sale of liquor throughout the province and a substantial source of provincial revenue. With prohibition abolished and Tom McKay elevated to his immediate superior in a re-organized police force, Rose resigned.

The Rose manuscripts are valuable historical documents on the prohibition period in Canada. Since most of the readily accessible material on prohibition was provided by the more articulate prohibitionists, historical accounts have tended to emphasize their perspective. Although stories of the "cops and robbers" games of the period are plentiful, most are difficult to authenticate.[30] It is rare indeed to find a frank and systematic explanation of how prohibition operated written by someone directly involved in its enforcement. Rose's unusual candour was a product of his literary ambitions and the progressive muck-raking tradition to which this work obviously belongs. His approach was effective not only in revealing the inner workings of prohibition and local politics but in shedding light on other topics. In his portrayal of his daily activities as constable, Rose frequently reminds the reader of the grim destitution faced by so many Canadians before the beginning of the welfare state, and he provides useful information on the social gospel, the Maritime Rights Movement, labour organization, the Ku Klux Klan, the status of Blacks and women, and other topics of social significance. And these are woven together in an entertaining yarn of detective work and political intrigue.

It is difficult to date Rose's autobiography with precision. He began writing an account of prohibition while still temperance inspector, but he dated the completed manuscript 1947. One suspects the wisdom of hindsight in comments upon the impact of the war on the Maritime economy and the stock-market crash. Nevertheless, a perusal of his diary suggests that the autobiography is an authentic portrayal of his ideas of the 1920s. It can be considered a largely contemporary account of events to which the diary provides a confirmation and supplement.

For reasons of space and cost, the editors have deleted from the autobiography an account of Rose's visit to the United States (renumbering the chapters) and from the diary most comments about the weather, books which Rose was reading, and the activities of his immediate family. All deletions are indicated in the text. In a few instances the editors changed names to initials where they judged their inclusion might cause embarrassment to surviving members of a family. Otherwise the original texts have been reproduced as faithfully and completely as Rose's sometimes indecipherable handwriting would permit. Copies of the complete texts, available at the libraries of Saint Francis Xavier University and the University of New Brunswick, are under the provenance of Mr. Garry Rose of Edmonton, Alberta. The editors would like to thank Mr. Garry Rose and his parents, Mr. and Mrs. Lincoln Rose, for making this publication possible.

NOTES

1 For an account of the prohibition movement in Nova Scotia see E.R. Forbes, "Prohibition and the Social Gospel in Nova Scotia", *Acadiensis*, I (Autumn 1971), pp. 11-36; and M.J. Strople (Campbell), "Prohibition and Movements of Social Reform in Nova Scotia, 1894-1920" (MA thesis, Dalhousie University, 1975). For general Canadian historical background on the period see R.C. Brown and Ramsay Cook, *Canada 1896-1921: A Nation Transformed* (Toronto, 1974).

2 Robert Wiebe, *The Search for Order, 1877-1920* (New York, 1967) is one of many useful analyses of progressivism in the United States. Interpretative surveys of the American literature on the topic are provided in D.W. Noble, *The Progressive Mind, 1890-1917* (Chicago, 1970) and O.L. Graham, ed., *Perspectives on 20th Century America* (New York and Toronto, 1973).

3 Ramsay Cook, "Henry George and the Poverty of Canadian Progress", *Canadian Historical Association Historical Papers*, 1977, pp. 143-56.

4 A.P. Reid, *Poverty Superseded: A New Political Economy* (Halifax, 1891).

5 *Year Book, Maritime Baptist Convention*, 1903, p. 22.

6 Richard Allen, *The Social Passion* (Toronto, 1971). See also E. Forbes' review article on *The Social Passion* in *Acadiensis*, II (Autumn 1972), pp. 94-9.

7 Early in the century most Roman Catholic social activity was justified in terms of the 1891 papal encyclical *Rerum Novarum*. For a later exposition of Social Catholicism see M.M. Coady, *Masters of Their Own Destiny* (New York, 1939).

8 A.A. MacKenzie, "The Rise and Fall of the Farmer-Labour Party in Nova Scotia" (MA thesis, Dalhousie University, 1969); David Frank and Nolan Reilly, "The Emergence of the Socialist Movement in the Maritimes, 1899-1916", *Labour: Journal of Canadian Labour Studies*, 4 (1979), pp. 85-113; J.K. Chapman, "Henry Harvey Stuart (1873-1952): New Brunswick Reformer", *Acadiensis*, V (Spring 1976), pp. 79-104.

9 V.J. Strong-Boag, *The Parliament of Women: The National Council of Women of Canada 1883-1929* (Ottawa, 1976): C.L. Cleverdon, *The Women Suffrage Movement in Canada* (Toronto, 1950). For

women's activity in Nova Scotia see especially the Halifax Local Council of Women Scrapbook, Public Archives of Nova Scotia.

10 Ian MacPherson, "Patterns in the Maritime Co-operative Movement 1900-1945", *Acadiensis*, V (Autumn 1975), pp. 67-83; L.A. Wood, *A History of Farmers' Movements in Canada* (Toronto, 1924), pp. 301-7.

11 The Nova Scotia Mining Society and the Halifax Board of Trade spearheaded the successful campaign for Nova Scotia's innovative programme of tenchical education. *Debates and Proceedings of the House of Assembly of Nova Scotia* [hereafter *Debates*], 1916, pp. 381-2.

12 For a typical review of the case against the liquor traffic, see E.H. Armstrong's speech, *ibid.*, 1907, pp. 305-15.

13 The Maritime Board of Trade took up the question in 1909. See *ibid.*, 1909, p. 342. See also MacLachlan's statement in the *Post* (Sydney), 19 October 1920. Labour was not united on the issue; see *Citizen* (Halifax), 15 August 1919.

14 *United Farmers Guide* (Moncton), 16 June 1920. The list of "principles" of the United Farmers of Nova Scotia for the guidance of candidates included "banning of the manufacture, import and sale of intoxicating liquor as a beverage".

15 *Report of the Royal Commission on Liquor Traffic*, 1895, pp. 76-87.

16 *Minutes of the Maritime Synod of the Presbyterian Church of Canada*, 1908, p. 25 and 1909, pp. 28-9.

17 J.K. Chapman, "The Mid-Nineteenth Century Temperance Movement in New Brunswick and Maine", *Canadian Historical Review*, XXXV (1954), pp. 43-60; P.B. Waite, "The Fall and Rise of the Smashers, 1856-1857: Some Private Letters of Manners-Sutton", *Acadiensis*, II (Autumn 1972), pp. 65-70.

18 R.E. Spence, *Prohibition in Canada* (Toronto, 1919), pp. 250-2.

19 *Debates*, 1914, pp. 725-8.

20 See Bulletins of the Council for Social Service of the Church of England in Canada, No. 12 "Reconstruction I" and No. 13 "Reconstruction II".

21 Nolan Reilly, "The General Strike in Amherst, Nova Scotia, 1919", *Acadiensis*, IX (Spring 1980), pp.56-77; Donald MacGillivary, "Industrial Unrest in Cape Breton, 1919-1925" (MA thesis, Univer-

sity of New Brunswick, 1971) and "Military aid to the Civil Power: The Cape Breton Experience in the 1920s", *Acadiensis*, III (Spring 1974), pp. 45-64; David Frank, "Class Conflict in the Coal Industry: Cape Breton 1922" in G.S. Kealey and Peter Warrian, eds., *Essays in Canadian Working Class History* (Toronto, 1976), pp. 161-84. See also Frank and MacGillivary's "Introduction" to Dawn Fraser, *Echoes from Labour's War: Industrial Cape Breton in the 1920s* (Toronto, 1976).

22 *Canadian Annual Review*, 1920, p. 681; Nova Scotia, *Journals of the House of Assembly* [hereafter *JHA*], p. 69.

23 E.R. Forbes, *The Maritime Rights Movement 1919-1927: A Study in Canadian Regionalism* (Montreal, 1979).

24 Report of Inspector-in-Chief for 1926, *JHA*, 1927.

25 *Workers' Weekly* (Stellarton), 26 December 1919.

26 See below, p. 63. Compare Rose's account with glimpses of the rum trade and system of enforcement in J.M. Cameron, *More About New Glasgow* (Kentville, 1974).

27 See Reports of the Royal Canadian Mounted Police, especially for the years ending 30 September 1921, p. 6; 1923, p. 17; and 1927, p. 43 in Canada, *Sessional Papers*.

28 See below, p. 64.

29 *Eastern Chronicle* (New Glasgow), 2 March 1928 and 8 January 1929.

30 *Cape Breton's Magazine* (Wreck Cove, Cape Breton), No. 11 [1975] records several interviews with rumrunners and enforcement officers who were active in the 1920s.

FOUR YEARS WITH THE DEMON RUM

1925 - 1929

by

CLIFFORD ROSE

DEDICATED

To the Saints and Sinners who fought and chased each other for the Demon Rum during the Roaring Twenties.

FOREWORD

It is customary when writing scraps of autobiography to develop at the outset some definite aim, purpose or intention for having the rashness to get down experiences and impressions in print.

Through the past years several of my friends have urged me to "write a book" on the tragedy, comedy and adventure of the days of prohibition. This wish has been carried out with the vain hope that readers may be entertained and catch the spirit of exhilaration in which we, the hunters and the hunted lived during the lush era before the Great Depression.

A second purpose has been to show from experience and by my crude reasoning the curse of party politics to life in my native province. Much has been said and written on this subject and it has been a political football for a long time because the loudest voices have been given to fools and they are the first to get the public ear.

Be that as it may, however, if from these pages some exiled Bluenose may momentarily catch the peculiar flavor of Nova Scotia; a flavor made up of the smell of the sea, the aroma of apple blossoms in June, the fragrance of pine sawdust, the sense of frustration arising from thwarted opportunity, the sunset from Green Hill, the taste of new maple sugar or the first trout in the spring, the bitter chilling April wind as it sweeps down from the Labrador, — these things go to make up a Down East impression that if aroused in some wandering fellow countryman to give him again the smell of home, I shall feel well rewarded and this labor has not been in vain.

CHAPTER I

The Search for Escape

"The trouble with you, Rose, is that you are too idealistic. You have been throwing energy and enthusiasm into fighting for the rights of the underdog while the 'wise' boys have been working for themselves. Now they can ride with their wives and sweethearts in cars while you have to hoof it and your wife and family have to thumb a ride or walk".

"I know it, A.J., I know, but if a fellow has something burning inside, if he sees the rights of Labor continually trampled underfoot, sees Greed going from victory to victory, it's fight we must. However, I'm beginning to see that this policy hasn't been playing fair with my family; but one gets into these things . . . ."

"Listen, Rose! don't be a sucker. Barnum correctly said, 'never give a sucker a break'. Abe Lincoln was an idealist and he got shot for his efforts. Now, listen, young man, in this depression-ridden province there are three industries open to the ordinary guy if he plays ball with the powers that be. These industries are lumber, politics and rum. All you know about lumber is to saw and nail it up for someone else. What you have learned about politics has been an eyeopener to oldline politicians. Speaking as your friend and as a politician of some experience, I can't understand how you fellows came so near to upsetting the established order with only one thousand dollars in your treasury and no rum to give the boys. You have something on the ball there. Now as for rum, I know you don't drink so you have missed a lot of fun. But at present time there is money in it, big money. Our industries are closing down, our young men are leaving in droves for the West and the States, — there is nothing for them to do here. Look at our bootleggers in shiny new cars eating up the dust on our highways. Do they carry a lunchbox? Not much; they can flash a roll and live at the best hotels. So wise up."

"A.J. I would jump into the West River before I would turn bootlegger."

"Now don't get hasty, I'm just giving facts and the setup of things as they are. Now what are the facts of this fight of yours for what you call 'the Rights of Man'. Four years ago the old corrupt Czar government of Russia blew up and a lot of long-haired guys the world over took it as a signal for world revolution. We hear strange battle cries about 'the Dictatorship of the Proletariat', 'Workers of the World unite, you have nothing to lose but your chains', You, along with the rest keep hooping [sic] it up."

"I know nothing about the Bolsheveki . . . ."

"Don't interrupt until I'm through. You along with the rest keep whipping up the storm to throw out our old established politicians. Now both you and I know that Germany hasn't been crushed. Our capitalistic system couldn't stand it. Sooner or later another big war is sure to come. The centre of this storm is in the same place that it has been for two thousand years — over in Europe. Here in Nova Scotia we are on the fringes, out in the sticks. The only time Nova Scotia has ever seen prosperity has been when there was a war. Halifax was built for war, thrives on war, geography takes care of that. Now that we are at peace depression is with us again. Building activities will soon cease and a carpenter with your reputation for Labor activities won't be able to get a job. Then what about your family and whose fault will it be if they are hungry and cold. You and your Labor Party can't stop injustice by making a pencil-mark on a ballot. If you believe that story you sure are a sucker."

The time was 1921, the place was the spacious veranda of A.J. Bannerman, successful lumberman and politician of New Glasgow and Barney's River in the County of Pictou. From the time he had been a country boy passing along Marsh Street to New Glasgow, he had admired the stately home of J. Fred MacDonald, Collector of Customs. With the passing years it had become a burning ambition to own that house, to be a prosperous citizen and live the life of Riley while directing his numerous enterprises. He loved the beautiful hardwoods of his Barney's River wood-lots and for many years had picked out choice boards, had them dressed and seasoned to adorn his prospective home.

With several successful lumber deals put through during World War I, he had bought the property and had hired some of us carpenters to panel the spacious halls and rooms with birdseye maple, ash and birch. A.J. prided himself on being a democrat and he was a colorful personality, and interesting talker. Our friendship has been long and lasting, something to be valued.

To get a clear idea as to how and why I became involved in the rum-running game it is necessary to give the background of what had been my experience in the class struggle.

I was born and lived as a boy on a farm on Fraser's Mountain just on the outskirts of New Glasgow. The scenery looking down on the East River, Pictou Harbour and the Cobequid hills beyond was and still is an artist's dream. My father, who although a poor farmer, was well-read and had something of the poet in him, for he loved to sit on the doorstep and look down to old Pictou and tell of the days when he could walk across the harbour on the decks of sailing ships as they awaited their turn to coal at the "loading ground" during the American Civil War. My mother believed in hard work and education for her children. It was a severe blow to her when I stopped school at Grade VIII. It wasn't that I couldn't learn for studies such as history, English or geography were more of a pleasure than a task. My refusal to go to school was the result of a perverse Highland pride stirred up because I couldn't dress as well as the town boys. On Christmas, 1903, my father presented me with a book that made a deep impression on my curiosity and imagination. It was a children's book of stories of the French Revolution. Why he ever picked that one as a Christmas present for a boy of fourteen is still a puzzle to me for he was a firm believer in God, the Queen and the "status quo". This old book is still in my possession and is something to be cherished: the Fall of the Bastille, the Insurrection of Women, the Six Hundred who knew how to die are stories more vivid than the seige of Stalingrad, El Alamein or the hanging of Mussolini. But greatest of all impressions was against the injustice and corruption of sanctified power. My greatest hero was Danton the Titan of the Revolution whose thunderous voice fired all France to hurl back the armies of Prussia, Austria and England.

Hail to thee Mighty Danton, thy strategy has saved me many, many times in the darkest hours. "Audacity, audacity and more audacity". It is a strategy that only can be called forth in grave emergencies. And it works.

I learned the carpenter trade, spending long hours at correspondence courses dealing with the building trades and drafting, joined the Carpenter's Union, served in its several offices. Through the Union we got better wages and shorter hours. A more conservative labor union is hard to imagine.

With the building of the Eastern Car plant in 1912, there came to Pictou County many workmen who had travelled widely and were real Reds. Some had belonged to the "wobblies" — the old I.W.W. — and the Western Federation of Miners. One such tough brainy son of toil was Cliff Dane an Australian boilermaker. He organized the American Federation of Labor and a Trades and Labor Council. The Carpenter's Union sent me as one of their delegates. From the literature passed around at Council meetings there dawned on me the first insight of the growing class-struggle.

During those formative years, Rev. A.J. Ramsay was minister at the Kirk. He organized a Brotherhood with a forum for discussion. He was a man who had qualities of tenderness and kindness; attributes of which I had known but little in my hard life. He must have sensed some glimmers of intelligence for he loaned books of immortal classics to me. These works piqued my curiosity to find out what springs of actions made people behave as they did. It was to be many a grim year before I could get a satisfactory answer to that question.

In those far off days before World War I it seemed to be a very good world in which to live, with those church discussions on Social Justice and Christian Socialism becoming a reality. Wanting to be on the "band wagon" of this millenium I threw energy and enthusiasm into making St. Andrew's Brotherhood a success. It was a fool's paradise in which we were living, it was little we knew or understood the strong currents that were running under our social structure.

Mr. MacColl, Superintendent of the Nova Scotia Steel & Coal Co. was the leading man in the church at the time and he gave it as his ruling that Socialistic discussions must cease. But my curiosity was whetted, I wanted to know more about the new horizons. So I attended every meeting of the Trades & Labor Council, coming to the conclusion that those rough-neck boys in those smoke-filled rooms had a better theory of the coming revolution than the good people in church parlors.

From such sources came the burning desire to fight the oppression of the capitalist. His sacred privilege of the right to plunder the masses must be taken from him. This was my fight so I threw energy and the best years of my life into the class war. During those years I saw many a good cause ruined by key men getting drunk at vital moments when they should have been sober. I was at one with the forces of temperance.

This struggle continued until 1920, when, as Secretary-Treasurer of the Labor Party we almost elected Henry D. Fraser. In fact on election night he was elected by a majority of 52. But through some skullduggery that could not be fathomed he was unseated next day.

This was the highpoint in my career in the struggle of the underdog to get his share of the gravy. After this crushing disappointment to the boys the recriminations flew thick and fast. Vannie Nicholson, an astute Labor leader and talker came to the meeting, three sheets to the wind, where we had to settle outstanding bills and demanded a recount of the ballots. I told him that our candidate had himself insisted that we drop the matter and take a trimming, and lashed out at him and others for getting drunk at the critical moment. It was a furious row. Next meeting was election of officers and I got fired. I walked out of that meeting and have never since gone to a Labor meeting.

During 1917 I got married to a smart attractive girl from Charlottetown, P.E.I., Bertha Garrick. To this day it is puzzling to know why she ever took such a crude bumptious fellow as I was in those days. We built a snug home, but it was mortgaged. When our two children were born I was forced to see that we would soon face disaster in the series of small depressions that were upon us. So I tried a small grocery store. But we had to buy in the dear market of inflation and sell cheap when the slump came. So we were cleaned out. There was little hope of getting out of the whirlpool of economic necessity by working at my trade and I was becoming despondent.

So my friend's advice to get into the rum trade was not to be lightly turned aside. But it was sickening to think of getting into the liquor traffic. One other thing I tried. Some friends believing there was some talent of self-expression lurking in my head persuaded me to try writing stories. What a laugh that one was! Anyhow several courses in English and story-writing were tried and I almost made good with a story sent to MacLean's magazine. The editor told me to see if I could repeat on another theme but it was just a fluke. Years afterwards I understood why I could never be a story-writer.

However, in all this welter of studying there was one chapter in one book that as I look back on it has amply repaid the effort. The chapter was on "Argumentation" from Gerung's *Outline of Rhetoric*. In all the mass of undigested books that had come my way this was the first time I had come across the scientific method of correct reasoning. It is hard to teach an old dog new tricks but through the succeeding years in my crude way this has been the method used to solve problems and satisfy curiosity on human behaviour.

CHAPTER II

The Sale of a Soul

Until 1925 rolled around I had tried several ventures to breach the wall of defeat that had piled around me. In the spring of that year another election for the Provincial House was necessary. People were stirred up about the conditions in the Cape Breton coalfields. Men who had served overseas were now behind trenches and barbed wire fighting company police. Ministers of the then Liberal government refused to go to the coalfields to see what the trouble really was. Instead more police were sent in and men were killed. The miners and their friends went around the country gathering produce to feed their starving families while the system of absentee ownership had Government approval.

The Conservative board of strategy at Ottawa sent down Edgar N. Rhodes to organize an effective opposition to the government that had been in power for over forty years. My political sense told me that Nova Scotia was due for a political turnover and as I had worked for the Tories in the old days it became my resolve to get in on the ground floor for whatever jobs were to be passed out with a change of Government. It needed the strangling of conscience and scruples to put me in the ranks of Tories as a mercenary, because I knew that one party was no better than the other. But the grim law of necessity and the hard facts of losing my home

and seeing my family destitute drove me along. "Audacity, audacity and
more audacity", Danton's battlecry, I took for mine.

My wife didn't want to me ever again mixed up in politics so I didn't
tell her that I was going to attend the Conservative Organization meeting
that April night. What a godsend I must have seemed to the Tory board of
strategy! Alex MacGregor — Big Alex as he was known — was the
commander-in-chief. James R. MacGregor was secretary. For short
to-the-point talks I had the knowhow to put fire and vigor into the crowd.
The Tory daily, the *Evening News* played it up in good style next day. Oh,
there was lots of ammunition in 1925 to throw at the Grits! The people
were sore.

Being called a renegade by old comrades was hard to take, but my
hand was set to the plough and there was no turning back. For me the only
alternative to the remote possibility of getting a government job was
failure and death.

In successful politics one of the tricks is to tell a half-truth loud and
long enough and the people will accept it for the truth. This strategy has
been worked over and over again yet the people go for it every time.

So this was the idea that I had to sell, that if a Labor candidate could
not be elected, the next best thing was to elect friends of Labor, thus the
miners could get a settlement and get back to work. Big Alex had proven a
friend of the workingman during the war years when he had obtained a
high rate for the steelworkers during the war. The thing to do was to
accept his party's candidates. Big Alex was astute and couldn't be played
for a sucker.

A theme I followed while stumping pleased him greatly. For years the
Grits of Nova Scotia had believed and had acted as though they had the
Divine Right to rule and own Nova Scotia. This attitude I kept hammer-
ing, and attacking again and again. Others took it up including the press.

Our candidates were John Doull, successful barrister and brother-in-
law of Big Alex; Allie MacQuarrie, merchant and prominent sportsman of
Westville; Robert Douglas, promising young farmer who had broken the
Grit strangle-hold on Granton in the municipal elections.

Fred Milligan, an old personal friend, was Ward chairman on the
West Side. Fred was a smart aggressive businessman and Town Councillor who had lived for a number of years in the States, and knew how to
hustle and get things done. In political action we could talk the same
language so that we helped each other heal many a sore spot. The old
diehard Tories in the fight were like all Tories, loyal to their class, forget-
ting nothing and learning nothing.

We were a motley lot of stumpers but we had a new line and didn't
resort to the old line of indulging in personalities. Our slogan was,

"Rhodes will bring the boys back home". The tide was coming in so we rode the crest of the wave. We had a lot of fun campaigning in remote hamlets and schoolhouses. Someone generally had a bottle of rum and although I didn't drink, it could be observed that there was great value in rum as a morale builder at elections.

There was an unforgettable moonlight night in June when we were returning from a meeting at the Garden of Eden schoolhouse in that gem of beauty at Eden Lake. Coming over Blue Mountain we stopped at a roadside spring with its trough hewn from a big log. The boys were mixing the drinks and I was drinking in the witchery and aroma of the woods when we heard the roar of a motor coming up the mountain from Sherbrooke. A big touring car passed us going at fifty miles an hour. "There comes some of our election rum", said one of the boys.

I asked Harry MacGirr who supplied the rum and as we were under prohibition, why it was that liquor Inspectors never touched us. Harry, being Irish and a natural politician, said, "Cliff, don't be so damned innocent. Election rum is like Holy Water. It is understood by all to be sacred stuff, not to be seized. Inspectors know that it must be left alone if they want to hold their jobs."

"Harry, do you believe that votes can be bought with rum?" "That is doubtful, but the workers must have it. The trick is to keep the gluttons from stealing it for their own use. This stunt makes the rest of the boys sore. The scavengers who hang around committee rooms are no good to the party or anyone else. Sooner or later as election day comes near you are sure to get your share of the rum. If you can't use it, others can. Being as you don't drink, you'll be trusted with two or three gallons. Water it down but leave the smell. That is too good for some of them."

Thus began my education in the ways and wiles of handling rum. How different from the puritanic Messiah-like campaign of the Labor party. True it was that Labor now had candidates in the field but it was pitiful to see their lack of steam.

There were amusing incidents aplenty. Some fights, for tempers ran high. Neil MacMillan a great Tory, kept a small store on High Street. For years I had made it a habit to drop in and have a chat. He had a lot of native Cape Breton wit and could tell a good story. The truckman who hauled coal in the neighbourhood was J.R. MacDonald, a fierce Grit from the Gulf Shore. One day when in Neil's store, J.R. came in and an argument started over an article in the Eastern Chronicle, the Liberal bi-weekly published by its noted editor, James A. Fraser.

Said J.R. "MacMillan, I'll be tellin' ye again that it was a MacDonald who wrote yon letter, The Honourable E.M. himself. I'll bet ye two dollars on it."

"Och, well now J.R. I holds no brief for James A. Fraser, but there was never a MacDonald could write like he can. And it's not bettin' I'll be on the likes."

The wild blood was aroused at this jab, as leaning across the counter, J.R. said, "Y're scairt, are ye"?

Neil was a stout man with great aplomb. Looking over his glasses he said with dignity, "Och, let me tell ye, MacDonald, I was placing bets an' winnin' them in the United States when ye were spreading manure with yer bare hands down the Gulf."

One of the most droll political speeches I've ever heard in my life was during that campaign by an old schoolchum, Bob Fraser. Bob was an electrician who loved to hobnob with the great and near great. They found him amusing and Bob's mind was a mirror for their thoughts.

On this particular night the meeting was in the schoolhouse at Marshdale at the headwaters of Barney's River. Bob began by saying, "Mr. chairman, ladies and gentlemen, I don't know if you know who I am but I'll tell you who I am. I'm Robert H. Fraser, the son of Jim Simon Fraser, a grandson of Yankee Tom a merchant known and respected throughout our province. The dearest and sweetest moments of my life have been spent in the arms of a nurse from Barney's River. But it is not of frivolous things that I came to talk about this evening, but of what happened when I was coming home from visiting my sweetheart the other night. Passing the home of a dear old lady, I heard sobbing. I went in to comfort her for her boys like your boys were driven out of Nova Scotia by the Grit Government. Said she, "oh Mr. Fraser, I'm so happy that I am crying. I've heard from my boys and they are coming home. God bless Mr. Rhodes, he is bringing my boys back home".

There was un unforgettable thrill to that campaign. Nevertheless sometimes I would lay awake at night and try to take stock of myself, knowing that Rhodes could never make good and "bring the boys back home", reasoning that neither he nor anyone else could break the tragic consequences of geography and stupid laws. At best a Tory victory could but break the Divine Right of Grit bureaucracy. To be honest with myself I was but a mercenary, conceiving my first duty to be to my family, to provide food and shelter for them. The scavengers that hung around the committee rooms were pitting their wits against the Executive to get a bottle of rum or five dollars for their vote. My purpose was different only in degree. But play the game I must and keep my big mouth shut against radical speeches. And never, never, never lie to myself.

As the eve of election drew near, the intensity of the struggle increased. Two nights before the climax Harry MacGirr took me aside and cautiously whispered, "Cliff, the time for talking is over. We must make our Ward solid. A prominent rumrunner has kicked in twenty kegs of rum to each party. Don't ask his name. We can't trust this Grit Inspector, Thompson. He isn't a gentleman. The town Inspector is O.K. He don't want to touch the Grit rum without Thompson getting nasty. So we have to do some scouting in cars to see that the distribution point is protected. We may work it so that Thompson will get drunk and carefully laid away. Be at the Market Square at ten-thirty tonight".

I'll admit that I was scared good and plenty for organized law-breaking had never been in my line, and a plausible story had to be told the wife about the purpose of the evening. She hated rum in all its forms and it was generally hard enough to get away to go stumping.

But there was a thrill and kick to the danger that lured me on. I asked the higher-ups in the party about the rum but they disclaimed all knowledge of such vile proceedings. I wondered about this paradox at the time but lost all such naive considerations later on in life. Liquor inspectors had a formidable reputation to me. I knew Tom MacKay slightly, Thompson only by reputation. He was County Inspector but had authority anywhere by virtue of holding a commission as a provincial constable.

It was this atmosphere that gave me the first inkling of the farce of prohibition. Was there no one in earnest about law enforcement. Was it but another pious dream getting kicked around by the natural cussedness of man?

But such moralizing must be forced to the back of one's mind. I was part of the machine and victory must be the only present objective.

At ten-thirty Harry and I circled the streets in a car belonging to one of the faithful. We picked up a good Tory cop who told us that Thompson was "up to Casey's", a celebrated joint run by an ex-painter who could not make a living at his trade. The cop told us to come around later and he should have further news. This was my first experience in stalking a human suspect and this one was a limb of the law. Later on we got a report that Thompson had a quart of rum and nothing was to be feared from his activities that night.

The distributing point was in the basement of a modest home. The tenants were socially prominent but unemployment had made the man of the house a seeker of a government job. The windows were covered with heavy cloth: a feeling of elation and coming victory filled the workers as they industriously filled the gallon cans. Cars came and went with party stalwarts from the country getting theirs first. Some one reported that the same thing was going on in a Grit hideout. I got three cans without trouble, a young chap and I went to his house and watered down two gallons pouring the ammunition into pint bottles. The other gallon we kept for election night celebration.

That June polling day dawned fair and bright. It wasn't necessary to buy votes, all we had to do was to keep the tide rolling. Grit workers surged around the poll with their air of Divine Ownership. It made one's blood boil and we worked all the harder. Deeds of valor were performed by men and women who had never before been interested in elections.

The people were aroused and showed it when the returns were added up. Each of our candidates had majorities of over three thousand. What a celebration we had that night. The Tories had been in the wilderness of opposition for over forty years so they had to make up for lost time.

In the midst of the delirium that night in the Arena Rink where the Tories had their headquarters, someone asked me as a leading ward-worker to make a speech. I was excited about the overthrow of the old government with their superiority complex and it made one feel good even if it was Tories that were taking over. It was the only radical statement made by me during the campaign. I said something about "it being the happiest work I had ever undertaken to take part in this victory in which the Grit aristocracy had been thrown to the dust and common man had come into his own". Big Alex got me in a corner later and slapping me on the shoulder said, "Clifford, that speech of yours was great". And he laughed long and loud, for he had little love for the established aristocracy, having made his way to the top by sheer ability.

CHAPTER III

The Valley of Humiliation

In the weeks that followed the change of government I was doomed to disappointment in getting a job. One thing that made me bitter was the fact that prominent job-holders under the Grit regime came asking me to use my influence to keep them in their soft jobs.

One day when I was getting building material in J.J. Grant's lumber yard my old friend A.J. Bannerman hailed me. He started away by saying "Cliff, this is the first time I've been around since election. Come on and have a drink. You sure gave us a h--- of a trimming. It is hardly possible that you came through that campaign without taking a drink".

"I did that, A.J. and I handled a lot of it. But now that the election is over there is not a man I'd sooner have a drink with than yourself even though I don't like the taste of rum".

"You'll have to learn to handle rum if you are going into politics. It is part of our lifeblood in Nova Scotia. Now that your feet are solidly on the Tory doorstep, get inside and rum is a good introductory card at any time."

Inside the shop of a prominent but thoroughly scared Grit bootlegger, we communed about electioneering. Into his ear I poured my story of disappointment in not getting a government job. He laughed, "Surely you don't expect one already. There is a Federal election coming on and they'll need you in that fight. So it wouldn't do to give you a job too soon. But make a nuisance of yourself without kicking over the traces, make a damned nuisance of yourself and afterawhile it will come. Good luck to you anyhow".

"Thanks, A.J., this rum is making my head swim, not being used to it. Thanks a lot". Thus with my old friend on that August afternoon I had my first drink of the fiery liquor, the liquor that was to put my feet on the road to economic liberty.

Sure enough, a Federal election was booked for the latter part of October and James R. MacGregor, the party secretary got after me again for service in the campaign. I haunted them as A.J. had suggested but beyond a politician's promise I could not get any satisfaction. At that time I had a steady job at my trade on the new Sharon Church and I had sense enough not to lose any time through politics without being paid. There was another phony battlecry being used by the Tories to get elected. They called it "Maritime Rights". Its deception was too strong for my blood so I steered away from that subject in any stumping that I had to do.

The reason for its deceit is that due to geography Nova Scotia is shut out of the markets of Central Canada, while because of high tariffs and aggregations of capital Maritimers are compelled to buy in a dear market. Thus year after year the common people get poorer and poorer. The only time that the shadow of prosperity crosses their threshold is when there is a war. Then due to Nova Scotia's strategic position, money flows into the Maritimes.

The platform of Maritime Rights that Tory politicians were saying they would put in force if elected, had an element of truth in it. But it would never be put into force because when elected, Maritime Rights would go the way of other election promises. Maritime Rights if enforced would mean that the rich central provinces would lose some of their markets and the rich boys behind the government who put up the cash for elections would not let that happen. These unseen forces control the heads of the Federal Government and these sources of visible power control the granting of Judgeships, Senatorships, Commissioners' appointments, etc. From the time each and every lawyer starts to practice, his eye is on a judgeship; [when he] gets married, gets into parliament and gets into the social whirl, a judgeship is deemed necessary to round out a well-lived life. If he ever had any genuinely patriotic ideas about Nova Scotia in his young life they would soon become submerged as he goes from triumph to triumph.

The same truth holds for any politician who comes back to the people and performs another sleight-of-hand trick and gets himself elected. He must play ball with the Premier who controls the good jobs and the Premier must play ball with the unseen forces that supply the money to win elections. So the whirligig goes on and on until the people start to think there can be no other answer. Oh Democracy, what crimes have been committed in thy name!

The Tories were elected by a small majority to the Federal House, Colonel Cantley being the elected Conservative in Pictou County. I worked at my trade most of that winter but my financial position was little better. I met Big Alex on Kirk Hill one day. He asked me how things were going as I had never bothered him about a job, never could see it as good strategy to do so. Somehow he seemed to understand men's motives. About a week afterwards I met Tom MacKay, town liquor inspector on the street. It was a damp snowy day in March.

"Doing anything now, Cliff"? "Not much, Tom. Things are very dull in my trade this time of year."

"Where can we go for a talk?" I suggested we go to the Odd Fellow's clubroom. It was empty so he laid before me the political setup. Attorney-General John C. Douglas had promised to vigorously prosecute the liquor traffic in the province. There was to be a prominent Temperance lawyer appointed as inspector-in-chief with several sub-inspectors under him. These Inspectors were to have wide powers, being provided with Writs-of-assistance — legal documents making possible raids on any house or premises by day or night. Needless to say such documents would only be given to men of proven discretion. The Attorney-General, John C. Douglas, was an exceptional politician and leader of men. His friends had a loyalty towards him that only an outstanding chieftain could obtain. Tom had got his political education under Douglas in Cape Breton when battle, murder and sudden death were no idle jests but grim facts. Tom told me that he was going to get the Deputy-Inspectorship for Eastern Nova Scotia and he wanted an Inspector in the principal town, New Glasgow, who could be trusted to play the party line. Although he did not say so, I gathered that the plan was to force the Trade and its ramifications under the control of the Conservative party. For years the Liberals had battened on the traffic now it must be shifted to Tory pockets. Besides, it had been found that since the elections some bootleggers were undermining the Tories' new-found power.

"Tom", I said, "courts are something I know nothing about. You know as well as I do that inspectors have been the butt and joke of press and pulpit for years. The strength of the Trade is so great that an ignoramus such as I am, would be kicked out inside of six months. That part of your proposition about driving the Grits from their fat jobs appeals to me. I'll have to talk it over with the wife. She has a horror of publicity such as I'll get from this."

"I'll have to know before the first of April for I'm going to try to take over as soon as the roads open. Have a talk with Fred Milligan and the Mayor. You know politics. This will be worth your while. As for being scared of the bootleggers, make no mistake about it, we are going after them; that is the only way to get them eating out of your hand. You have a lot to learn. Common sense is all you need. Also your days of talking on a platform are over if you get this job where your tongue is like fire, — a good servant, but a bad master."

"Well, Tom, believe me I'll be glad of the day when I'll stop stumping. I'm sick of this talking about what I don't believe. I'll let you know by Saturday night."

The upshot was that after much backroom log-rolling on April 7th, 1926, the headlines announced, "Ex-labor leader appointed N.S.T.A. Inspector."

CHAPTER IV
Into the Swim

It was a pitiful and forlorn inspector who put in his appearance at the town office to be sworn in. Tom came with me for moral support, then took me to the Police Station and introduced me to the Force. Now it must be remembered that up to this time courts and the Law were as foreign to me as the moon. I was suspicious of and had a dread of lawyers and policemen. My wife was sceptical and opposed to this way of making a living, if living it could be called; seventy-five dollars a month was to be my salary for a start. How the authorities ever expected a man to be honest to the Law and to himself is a deep question, without the prima facia statement was accepted that the Inspectorship was a farce.

However I was determined be my tenure of office long or short, I would be no farce. If the semi-criminal wise-guys thought me a "fish" and a gullible fool, — well let them dream until my feet set. Then would be called into play the strategy learned from the old book on the French Revolution, "audacity, audacity and more audacity". This was something hard for them to understand except in results.

In the modern control of liquor there is no parallel office to the Nova Scotia Temperance Act Inspectorship. An Inspector to be successful had to be a mixture of lawyer, policeman, politician, fox and lion; and on top of that he had to have the element of luck.

As I re-read my old notebooks of those early days the memories come crowding back and it is difficult to adjust a starting point so that a correct sequence to four years of adventure, comedy, danger and tragedy may be recorded. This is but the record of a mercenary who played the game to bring his family and himself out of the shadow of debt and destitution but as Shakespeare said, "there is a special Providence in the fall of a sparrow". Although never a healthy or rugged individual yet I was in the prime of life, if I had any creed it was to live and let live.

Pitted against me were the resources great and strong of the Trade. I knew that the good wishes and prayers of many a starved wife and mother were with me for rightly or wrongly I had a reputation for decency. Clergymen told me that they would give me every assistance.

During that first day as Inspector, Chief-of-Police "Woody" Osborne took me into his office to give me some advice that was good and gave me confidence. "Cliff, you have lived a clean life; I have looked the seamy side square in the face. Make it a point to do your duty and don't be a goat for anybody. Anytime you want assistance from the Force, don't be afraid to call us day or night. Don't tell your business to outsiders. We must all stick together for the Force is the target of unjust abuse".

I had much the same advice from old and respected Archie Nickolson. He had been connected with Pictou County police work for over fifty years.

Another man who had his say to me regarding prohibition enforcement was my neighbour, John Calkin. John was the nearest thing to being a Christian of any man I had ever met. He had tried his hand at liquor inspector two years previous and had given it up in disgust because the men who should have supported him failed to do so in decisive moments.

Listening to these various advisors caused battle-lines of friends and enemies to be formed in my mind. It hit me with a wallop that in this business one could not get anywhere without friends.

The prosecuting lawyer was a Liberal, Rod G. MacKay, "Rod G." as he was known in police circles. Tom advised me that Rod G's law was sound. The lawyer of the Trade was generally R. Douglas Gbrame, [Graham] a clever criminal lawyer and prominent Liberal who seemed to have the bootleggers under his thumb. The Magistrate was D.C. Sinclair of an old established Liberal family.

Some twenty-five years previous we had gone to the same school but in the meantime there had been no occasion for us to exchange words. The prohibition forces called him all sorts of names. Drunks and sinners said, "he'd give a guy a break". Police and lawyers were afraid of him. So it was with apprehension that I approached him to have twenty-five search-warrants signed.

"Some search-warrants to be signed, Mr. Sinclair", I said, being resolved to keep my mouth as tightly closed as possible. He signed them, said nothing and went on reading the Halifax Chronicle.

To write of the Trade in the Roaring Twenties is to mention rum most frequently. The reasons for this is that rum could be smuggled ashore much more profitably than whiskey or gin. The profit in rum was immense, West Indies rum being capable of absorbing a lot of water. It was also easy to handle coming in ten-gallon kegs capable of rough usage. Rum also suits the damp foggy Nova Scotia climate.

At that time the advent of a new Inspector sent a thrill of fear through the little underworld of our town. The dives closed up solid, Tom told me that they wouldn't re-open until the grapevine reported my behaviour.

Tom and Jim Caldwell, the senior officer of the force, took me around on a series of raids. I was amazed and astonished at the number of joints, at the squalor of some, at the opulence of others, at children being brought up in an atmosphere of crime.

"Tom", I asked, "why don't bootleggers with children get away from this life of crime?"

"Where could they go? What else could they do that would give them the easy money they get out of selling a gallon of rum? And don't forget the sociability that goes with bootlegging helps bind them to this kind of life."

"In other words, empty stomachs and the boredom of life are the causes of bootlegging?"

"Correct. But don't get to thinking about causes, these things have been going on for a long time. Without bootleggers we wouldn't have jobs. And your job is to get convictions. If you scare the Trade too much there will be no convictions to get. We can't afford to kill the goose that lays the golden egg. The Chief tells me that one of the officers is sick tonight. You take over for the shift and learn for yourself what is going on."

It is hard to describe the mixed feelings of awkwardness and fear that took hold of me as I tramped the streets of my home town as Liquor Inspector that April night. All kinds of gang warfare and killings rushed through my mind. But Officer MacCann was a stout fellow and steered me in the right directions.

It had been a long cold winter with lots of snow and as yet Spring had brought few thaws to melt the banks of snow and ice in backyards and alleys. Casey's was a famous joint in those days. It was on the second floor of a building next to the Norfolk Hotel. It had the reputation of having more "Hides" than any other dive in town. On the back there was an open balcony without a stair to the ground and during the winter Casey had shovelled the snow until it made a heap that I thought was high enough to stand on and pull oneself up to the balcony. I suggested this idea to MacCann. He said he was too heavy weighing over two hundred pounds but said as I was more wiry I could throw off my overcoat and try it, keeping as quiet as possible. This we tried and I pulled up MacCann. We crept close to the window and through it was my first glimpse at the gay life. Casey kept his place clean as his patrons were of a better class than the joints across the track. Being close to the town's best hotel, the guests used it as a place to have the odd drink with friends. Casey's wife, Hilda, was known to be an able dealer. When customers got too drunk to notice her move she served them black tea as rum at twenty-five cents per small glass.

Beside the sink laughing and carousing were three travellers and two ladies of pleasure above the grade of street-walkers. The rum that Hilda served them came from a pitcher that she constantly watched. MacCann and I considered whether the kitchen door was locked. Quietly I turned the knob then pushed. Glory be! Lady Luck was with us, the door opened. We rushed to the sink but Hilda was to quick for me but one of the travellers left his half-filled glass of rum that I grabbed. MacCann ran to the door that led to the street, telling all the "guests" to stay where they were. As Tom directed I took the names and addresses of all present. There were several patrons in the different rooms, one man high in the ranks of the Liberal party. This looked to me like good pickings.

After having a sleep next morning, I looked up Tom with the intention of telling him about the raid but the street was buzzing with the news of the raid and the audacity of the method used.

"Catching that old Grit buzzard in Casey's is worth a lot to me. He was the man that had me fired as County Inspector. He is a deacon and I wonder how he will like getting a summons served on him and appearing in court with those two broads. Good work, Cliff, good work".

But no one had to go to court for that raid. Casey came down to the Police Station, pleaded guilty and was fined "Two Hundred dollars and costs".

It was my first victory and my friends were well pleased. The Evening News spread the headlines for in those lively days of the "Roaring Twenties", prohibition all over North America was the foremost topic of conversation. From New York to New Glasgow the ferment bubbled and foamed. The white light of publicity beat upon the forces of enforcement. I have seen some men go raving crazy through the talk of it.

Then there were the women. If a cop with a roguish fearless twinkle in his eye keeps his clothes snappy and clean and "gets around", some women are sure to take a lot of risks on the chance to get into his arms. It matters not their rank or station for Judy O'Grady and the Colonel's lady are all the same under their skin.

This twisted female thinking happened a few days after the Casey raid. We raided a homebrew joint run by a woman about whose conduct several complaints had come to the police. We found a lot of rank homemade beer and had it analyzed by a chemist who found that it had an alcohol content of 5%. She was arrested and locked up. Before the trial she sent word she wanted to see me. Whispering through the bars of her cell she said, "Mr. Rose, I have a pretty daughter of seventeen. If you will let me off I'll give you a note to her and you can take her out. She's O.K.".

I didn't avail myself of the opportunity so she went to jail for three months. Some time later the daughter was pointed out to me and she was pretty.

On one of those April days the Mayor, J.J. Fraser, phoned me to say that Rev. Dr. Grant was at his store and wanted to talk to me. "This is it," I said to myself. At that time the Rev. H.R. was the head of the Moral Reform forces in Nova Scotia being their Secretary. His letterheads were a fearsome thing suggesting the tramp of Onward Christian Soldiers. In his younger days he had been quite an athlete and there was no questioning his courage.

I knew the Mayor to be a good business man, shrewd, wanting to make a record of good administration for his tenure of office. He introduced me saying, "that he was sure I could learn much from Dr. Grant's experience".

He questioned me as to drinking habits and familiarity with bootleggers, cautioning me "that their polish and niceness were but cloaks to cover their deception of frail humans who were beguiled by such devilish pleasantries".

Said he, "I have two names of men who have come forward and are willing to buy liquor from the bootleggers and go on the witness stand and swear to it".

"You would have me commit a crime to catch a crime?"

"It is no crime to do anything legal to help stamp out the accursed Traffic".

"I cannot see it that way, Dr. Grant. The bootleggers are dealing in an illegal article. If I am lucky or smart enough to catch them at it they are going to be chased hard and fined".

"But I don't want them fined, I want second-offences laid against them. This fining is only a license system".

"You are advocating a course that would soon put me back at sawing boards for a living and temperance would be no further ahead. My intentions are to lead a decent life at this business and make good".

Here the Mayor cut in, "Cliff, I want you to cooperate with Dr. Grant in the prosecution of the liquor Traffic. Get together and work out a plan". That settled the conference. I knew from a close friend in the Council that their attitude as a whole was for the town to get from the trade all the money it could for civic purposes. The councillors were practical men anxious to do all they could for the town. So from that angle I had little to fear in being reprimanded. However, this business of being an agent provocateur seemed to be bad in itself.

That night I looked up Officer MacCann and suggested that we go down and raid "Dannie". For "down to Dannie's" was a famous term used by drinkers who came to town. Although I had never spoken to Dannie MacLennan, his reputation had for years been dinned into my ears as being a man who only lacked the horns and hoof to make him the devil. For three generations the MacLennans had sold rum in New Glasgow with the laws getting stricter all the time. But Dannie had never a conviction registered against him. He was reputed to be worth a sum in six figures; was a force in politics and the detection of crime. He kept a crowd of destitute has-beens eating from his table, had his finger on the pulse of all activities that would be liable to affect his business and had amongst business men the reputation for being "wise".

"Down to Dannie's" was across the railroad track on Kempt Street. It was a big rambling house that exuded an air of mystery as forms silently shuffled away in the darkness. I had not come down with the expectation of making a haul but wanted to familiarize myself with the famous place and its host. MacCann advised me, "go right in the front door, it won't be locked. I've been here often before I went on the Force".

Sure enough the door was open and Dannie's brother, "Buttons" came from a side room. Years ago we had gone to the same school. "Hello, Cliff, haven't seen you for years. You want to see Dan? I'll get him for you. And how are you Enoch? I've got something for you on the Burnette case. Step this way to Dan's office. He'll be down in a minute".

Scarcely had we made ourselves comfortable in huge easy chairs when Dannie slipped in. He was smooth even in his walk.

"Good evening, Enoch. Our new Inspector, Cliff Rose? So glad to be in when you called. Make yourselves comfortable or do you want to look the house over?"

"That is what we came down for, Dannie, but it isn't hard to see that you haven't anything in. I thought this would be as good a time as any to get acquainted".

"Right you are. Things have been quiet down here since you moved in. Strange for us to have lived in the same town and never to have met. It has come to my ears that you are a serious man who never had much fun in your life, that kind of an Inspector is dangerous to my business. But you'll find as you move around that it is better to learn to laugh. If Dan

MacLennan stops selling rum someone else will start. It is all a game, every man plays it from his own corner, even Dr. H.R. Grant. All we ask is that you play the game fair. If you catch us, we'll pay up. I know that the councillors want all the money they can get for civic purposes. In order to survive we must be able to change with the changing conditions. Have you ever gone fishing in your life".

"Not since I was a boy".

"You'll have to learn, Cliff. It mellows one's life and is good for the soul."

"As soon as the roads open I intend to get a rod and line and wet them. But as regards the enforcement of the law, it's the man who pays the fiddler who calls the tune. No one except Dr. Grant wants to hear about second offences in liquor cases. What do you think about it?"

A fleeting moment of hostility, then the pleasant urbane face lit up with a smile as his dark eyes danced with mirth. He was thick-set of medium height with long fingers that spoke of familiarity with pool and billiards.

"Prosecutions for second offences mean a fight for every first offence. The law entanglements that would follow if the boys in the Trade put their heads together wouldn't look good to the town council. To be sure none of us like to pay two hundred dollars and costs but we take that risk."

"Well, Dannie, I'm glad we called. We will look the house over. There is something about this place that tickles my fancy".

Dannie came with us and showed every possible courtesy as we looked for hides. He was a smooth actor alright and I told MacCann so when we got outside.

"He's smooth, alright, but that's a laugh when he says he is not selling. Does he think we are a bunch of rubes? He has three joints selling for him on George Street. The one upstairs is the slickest. You'll have to go some to get that one. Those old bums that live off Dannie carry the rum in cans, but try to catch one of them, they are watching all the time".

Next day was Saturday, payday at the Steelworks and mines. Early in the morning I looked over Dannie's building on George Street. There was a stair to the second floor at the back of the building. Otherwise there was little chance of getting in. Several complicated schemes went through my mind but experience told me that for me audacity was the best strategy. So at noon hour I climbed the board fence at the back of the building and waited until three men in working clothes went in. They seemed to get in without any trouble. Slowly I sauntered over and climbed the stair and opened the door. It was a daring stunt, afterwards Tom MacKay told me never to try it again.

Several men were in the room. The sink and pitcher of rum were there just as it had been explained to me. One man, an old printer that I had known in labor union days yelled to the proprietor but I had that pitcher and was out the door before they realized that a serpent was in their midst. The surprise had stunned them. Believe me, I was glad to be on the street again. Town authorities had given me a cell to store evidence and two expensive locks to protect it. The success of this raid puffed me up somewhat.

I had expected to have a big trial, but that evening Officer MacCann told me that "Dannie had given his bartender Hell for being careless and that the fine would be paid as soon as the papers were served if it could be arranged in the Magistrate's office."

This unexpected turn of event suited me fine. All the boys on the force told me that I would get a bad tumble if I had taken it to open court. This could well be believed, so the town was two hundred dollars richer. Walter Weir was chairman of Police and a squareshooter. "Rose", he said, "If you keep up that clip we'll raise your salary right away". And they did.

Dannie's personality and power aroused my curiosity and I lost hours of sleep trying to correctly assess the facts. Dr. Grant wanted me to use spies to catch men who were living by an illegal game forced on them because of economic necessity and the boredom of life. Dannie MacLennan suggested that it was all a game. If all hands played fair he was sport enough to ante up when caught. Plainly, these bootleggers had a code of honor. Were the "bad" men good and the "good" men bad? That would be a subject for mental investigation on dull days when things were quiet.

Then there was his remark, "in order to survive we must be able to change with changing conditions". The more one conned it over the more the truth of it sank in. Yes, I would put that slogan on a signpost in my mind for dangerous corners.

Magistrate Sinclair had a stromy brow when he tried the case of Dannie's bootlegger in his office, and it didn't improve matters any when the accused pleaded "guilty". Saying nothing I walked out of the office with the money in my pocket but felt that there was a storm around my head.

Amongst the many "retail" bootleggers of that time was Newman Betts and his wife Liz. They lived in the old Captain Walker house near the East River, a house that had been a palatial residence in the days of Nova Scotia windjammers. Another tenant was "Pitcap" Dan MacDonald and an old girl he had living with him. Sometimes "Pitcap" went away on weekends and his girl took in another man. On one such Saturday she took in Duncan MacKenzie. Duncan MacKenzie bought a quart of rum from Liz to make merry that pay night. He was in the big pay brackets in the steel plant and had a roll of two hundred and fifty dollars on him but awoke on Monday morning broke; he had been rolled.

Such victims receive scanty pity from police but they must do their duty. While Duncan had been getting the rum an Indian had also [been] seen buying a pint. This Indian was arrested for being drunk that Saturday night but hesitated to tell where he got the firewater. When Duncan told his story he also told about the Indian getting the rum.

There are severe penalties provided in the Indian Act for anyone who sells liquor to an Indian. There is also a provision that gives the informant half of the fine. Rod G., my lawyer, saw a chance of a prosecution under this act with the consequent large fees paid by the Department, so we decided to go after Liz under that law. I was to be the informant.

We got out a warrant for her and when Magistrate Sinclair signed it he looked grimmer than ever, asking the question, "Why are you taking her up under the Indian Act"?

"On the advice of my lawyer".

"Does the Town Office know about this?"

"Not yet".

"Well they will". The town clerk, James Roy, was very zealous about getting all the money he could for the town and the idea of two hundred dollars going to Ottawa was hard to swallow. The town clerk sent for me and gave me quite a lecture. But I shut him off with the remark, "that there was lots of money where that came from".

When the chairman of police heard about it he laughed and told me not to let it happen again. But it got under my skin to have this skullduggery going on behind my back. I was new at the game and was thinskinned.

Liz was arrested, pleaded "guilty" and was fined two hundred dollars and costs. The joke in the affair was that Duncan lost his case and we later heard by grapevine that Liz had known about the "rolling" when Duncan and his girl were asleep. It was Duncan's money that paid the fine. It took three months to get my share of that money from Ottawa and even then I had to write Colonel Cantley our Federal member to intervene to get it. Someone had tried to spike my gratuity.

That month of April, 1926, must have been one of the worst on record. The account of the breakup of the ice in Pictou Harbor sets it down as April 26th of that year. On one snowy slushy morning while Tom and I were sitting in the police office we got a hot tip that seven barrels of beer were coming into the freight shed. Tom told me that he didn't have his papers as yet and it would be better for me to make the seizure and have it locked in the cell.

When we got to the freight shed the seven barrels of beer were there. I declared them under seizure but the station-master said that the C.N.R. didn't come under the jurisdiction of the N.S.T.A. Not being sure of my legal ground we left Officer Caldwell sitting on one of the barrels while I looked up Rod G for law. It must be remembered that in those days no police officer in New Glasgow had a car so we had to plough through snow and slush.

Rod G looked up the law and found that the railroad came under the Canadian Temperance Act so a search warrant was made out accordingly. I had to go to Magistrate Sinclair's office to have it signed. He was home to dinner by this time and told me on the phone that he would be over when he got good and ready. By this time I was getting hungry, cold and mad and knew that Officer Caldwell sitting in the draughty freight-shed would be the same. I called a taxi — a brazen thing for an officer to do in these days — and had to sit until 2 p.m. until the Magistrate arrived at his office. Keep my temper I must even though he delivered me a tirade on the "gaul" of officers and Rod G's law.

If the Magistrate was cross the old Station-master was raving mad. He swelled up as though he would die of apoplexy. But we loaded the beer on a truck and hauled it to the jail. It was big news for the papers and we got the headlines in great shape.

With Chief-of-Police Osborne I talked over the matter of the Magistrate's hostility. He told me that this attitude was old stuff with him, but I had now a lever with the Inspector-in-Chief, D.K. Grant. The N.S.T.A. could never be enforced if, prima facia, police officers were to [be] treated as criminals. He advised me to write the Inspector-in-Chief stating the facts. After some misgivings this was done and soon had results.

The Magistrate cornered me in the police station for informing against him. Respectfully, I told him that all I wanted was fair play and not to be looked upon as a malefactor until such had been shown to be the case. From that date onward I found him to be fair, sometimes he decided against me but that was to be expected. His attitude towards criminals was that of British law, "a man is innocent until he is proven guilty".

One fine May day Liz Betts approached Officer Langille asking protection·from her husband while she removed the furniture. She had got tired of living with him and had found a man more to her liking. I went along with the officers and there was Newman stretched across the bed, drunk. She grabbed the mattress dumping Newman onto the floor. He cursed and babbled about her infidelity. She knocked the bed apart and threw it downstairs. Then she took the pitcher and basin of the toilet set and set them in the hall. When she came back Newman was on one elbow, saying, "My God, Liz, leave me the thunderjug".

The weather broke nice and fine in May and I felt that it was good to be alive. Truly, nothing succeeds like success. I got a commission as Provincial Constable and Tom MacKay took me along in his new car on raids throughout his district. Sometimes Pearle Bailey, assistant Customs collector and interested in liquor smuggled without paying duty, also came along. I thought that I was learning fast but a lot of it was just the luck that goes with an amateur's audacity. From lawyers I got constable work that paid well and for the first time in my life found ready cash in my pocket.

My first fishing-trip with the gang was to Fisher Archibald's lake in the backwoods of Guysboro County. It is a big lake on the headwaters of the St. Mary's River. There is a walk of some three miles to the lake but that only added to the fun. After all those years of toil and treadmill struggle it was like being wafted to another world to arise early that first morning in the shack while the fog was still on the water; to smell the fresh damp moss and get the aroma of wet hemlock; then back to the camp and sit down to a breakfast of bacon and eggs washed down with hot strong tea and a dash of smuggled rum. Good old rum, my emancipator! So long as I live I'll never forget the call of the loon that first misty morning on Archibald's Lake.

CHAPTER V

Through the Woods

Coming back to town, temperance enforcement had a different meaning. Now Dannie's reference to it as being a game could be understood. A grim game it was for Officers Langille and MacCann.

There were several joints run by women at the time known to patrons as "Mothers". Mother Robertson had a bouncer, one Jimmy Johnstone from Springhill. He was an ex-miner, tough and hard. One Saturday night he was creating a disturbance on Front Street and the officers were sent to arrest him. They had to use their billys freely and he was a bloody mess when he landed in jail. Mother Robertson hired R. Douglas Gbrame [Graham] to prosecute the cops for beating up her bouncer and they were sent to Supreme Court for assault. They were let out on bail and Walter Weir, Chairman of Police stood right behind them.

They watched her joint like hawks and one night when we were sure there was rum inside we pulled a raid in fine style. Doors went down like ninepins. Customers, white as sheets were herded and searched and we got considerable rum. Mother was arrested and locked up. She got out on bail and a date was set for the trial. I had been seven weeks on the job and had got several convictions without a fight in the courts.

There was a big audience for the trial as Doug Grahame had quite a reputation as a criminal lawyer and the fight between the cops and the underworld was becoming common gossip. That was my first experience on the witness stand and Doug Grahame went after me in grand style. But having stood up to some stormy sessions in the Labor movement this cross-questioning did not, as Rod G. put it, "turn a hair on your head".

We got a conviction and the old girl had to fork over "two hundred dollars and costs". It was not the money so much as the prestige it gave the police force that mattered in that vital case, for Mother Robertson had been defiant and the repercussions did a lot to clear the officers when they went on trial before a jury.

That trial also knocked the pins from under the strong hold the Liberal machine had on the Trade, so, for the next two years the local Tories held sway. I got several approving remarks from the temperance workers and the Mayor was well pleased. Even James Roy the town clerk thawed enough to smile when I went into the town office.

The weather had become fine and hot and the tramping around on foot was making things tough and unpleasant. I envied Tom MacKay and Pearle Baillie travelling in their cars so the idea came to me to get one also. The wife and family were also of the same mind. She had saved a few dollars and agreed to put it into part payment of a car. The Mayor went on a note for me at the bank and the finance corporation took up the rest.

I bought a Star touring car, used to get thirty miles to the gallon and have never got such service from any car since. The charges of grafting that were now levelled [at] me were furious for seldom had a man in straitened circumstances on the small salary of ninety dollars per month blossomed out with a new car in two short months.

Complaints were made to the councillors but they knew the rights [of] the story, so in the leafy month of June, 1926, that Star could be seen on the highways with the Inspector's family and friends going to places I had never expected to see in my life.

One of the first trips I had was to take my mother to have a look at the old home in which she was born. Those grand people of that old generation had an attachment to the home and soil that must have come from Scotland. It is hard to get the present generation to understand that such a thing ever existed. My mother was pleased and happy at that simple experience.

At that time the by-roads were just beginning to be graded and opened up for cars. Lawyers gave me a lot of constable work and it wasn't long until that note was paid at the bank. Oh, it was grand that experience of driving along freshly graded roads with the smell of the sea and damp earth in one's nostrils. There was sunshine in my heart and the blood sang in my veins as we often drove along the Shore road to Antigonish on that drive of surpassing beauty.

One such drive I particularly remember. I had often wanted to see the Gulf shore after a Nor'easter. We had had quite a blow towards the last of June and as luck would have it I had some legal papers to serve at Merigomish. After serving them I kept on going towards what was to me unexplored country, past the good farms of Big Island, the Ponds and Lismore where the Gaelic is still spoken to the wild rugged country of Arisag. Here the wheel track wound perilously near to the hundred foot cliff above the sea. Parking the car, I got out. "Here", I said, "This is it".

Such wild forbidding beauty I had never seen, as I pinched myself to be sure it wasn't a dream. There at my feet the rollers surging down from the Labrador were breaking and tossing their salt spray in my face. Down to my right on wild rocky Arisag point the lighthouse was often drowned in the spray even in that bright sunshine that had followed the storm. To my left a small waterfall murmured between the crash of the breakers and a cowbell tinkled on the mountainside behind me. How long I stayed there I do not know as it was hunger of the body that pulled me away. For hours afterwards I was dazed by the impact of such wild beauty so near to my home. Poets and writers have written about the Annapolis Valley and the Bras D'or Lakes but surely the finger of Deity was just as evident on the Gulf Shore as on those famous landscapes.

It was after seeing that and subsequent scenes of Nova Scotia's beauty that I began to ponder the causes of the poverty of my countrymen living with such natural advantages and scenic beauty. But it was to be many, many years of experience and reasoning before a satisfactory answer could be obtained to that problem.

CHAPTER VI

A Closeup on Squalor

During the month of July Tom MacKay took me along on many a trip of adventure in the enforcement of the N.S.T.A. One such trip was to Gairloch in the heart and hills of Pictou County. "As big as the church at Gairloch" had been an expression of the old people when they wanted to describe anything of great size. There on a hill it stood, majestic though weather beaten. What tales could be told of its sacraments in Gaelic and English. Not far away is Gairloch Lake nestling by the roadside. Through emigration the surrounding farms had been largely deserted and the manse had fallen into neglect with grass and weeds growing in its walk. A new minister Rev. D. MacKinnon from Cape Breton, had taken charge. Being a carpenter before he became a preacher, he set about repairing his home.

He had complained to Tom about the selling of beer by two sisters with several illegitimate children. In their childhood these sisters had been orphaned and had grown up neglected and the object of the lust of men. They lived in an old unpainted farmhouse with most of the cellar wall having fallen in.

Sometimes dances were held in the bare parlour and sordid affairs they must have been. On the day previous to one of these dances we pulled the raid. About fifty bottles of homebrew were secured as the house was searched. As we broke it the smell of the stuff made me retch. It was little use bringing the girls to trial as they had no money to pay a fine and to send them to jail would be to have left that unhappy brood to the care of the overseers of the poor. Nobody wanted that to happen.

During the search of the second floor on the back of an unpainted bedroom door in lead pencil was written a list of men's names with X's in front of them. I called one of the sisters and asked her for the explanation.

Said she, "My sister, Mary, died of consumption in this very room. That is the list of men who loved her and how often".

One of the interesting trips I had that summer was with Tom and Walter Weir to the Dover Picnic in Guysboro County. The Parish priest had complained to the Attorney-General about hooligans spoiling the affair for his people and he wanted protection. In those days no permanent police force was required in municipalities so Tom was notified to police the picnic.

This was the first extensive drive I had ever had into remote corners of Nova Scotia and in those days when the roads were just beginning to be opened for motor traffic the outing had a spice of adventure. We had dinner at Mulgrave then started the long drive across the rocky barren hills over-looking the Strait of Canso. On the other side lay Cape Breton the storied island of romance. It was on those long trips that we all learned from one another so many songs, Gaelic and English, that we sang to pass the time. Tom would stop his car at some remote farmhouse, saying, "that's where Captain So-and-So lives. He is quite the smuggler. Let's give him a raid". Beyond getting a bottle of Scotch at one house that trip was barren of catches.

In the low second-floor attic of one house at Pirate Cove in an old trunk I found an eight-day clock made in the States around 1870. These clocks had been peddled around Nova Scotia and a home without one was something the same as a home today without a car. I bought the clock for four dollars, spent thirty on it to be put in shape and still have a great time-keeper and a beautiful clock. Twenty-four hour clocks were common but eight-day clocks were and are scarce.

The poverty of the people in those little villages along the coast was pitiful. Not so much squalor as to be seen in the towns but the children seemed to be under-nourished and tubercular. We took our time going down that wild stretch of coast getting into Canso in time for supper. We looked up political friends who gave us the "low down" on the picnic and the Trade. Canso is a cable town built on a point jutting out into the Atlantic and leaves a memory of a strong smell of fish. Along the rocky coast the ocean seems to brood over its next spell of anger when it will hurl its might against the gigantic rocks studding those inhospitable shores.

Next morning we started for Dover. Going back four miles on the highway we branched off for a seven mile drive over the bare rock to the little village where the picnic was being held. What infinite variety of scenery has Nova Scotia. The pleasant farmlands of Antigonish and Pictou seemed to be thousands of miles away. Here all was stark naked barren and terrible. Rocks the size of houses had been tossed about by some upheaval of Nature millions of years ago.

A few weather-beaten houses, a fish house on a wharf with some boats, lobster traps, a store, these along with the little white chapel on the hill, — that was Dover. Some years later the extension department of St. Francis Xavier University took the adult education of the village in hand and transformed its character. But when we were there the community had a hung-dog look. On a big rock near the harbour's mouth a seal was disporting himself. With my revolver I fired at him but his hoarse bark might have been a laugh at my marksmanship as he plunged into the Atlantic.

If the surroundings were inhospitable the hearts of the kind folk of the parish opened to us. In the basement of the chapel a great feast was spread but we didn't sit down to eat until the village bootlegger was raided. He had in his possession some rum and a quantity of beer in readiness to liven up the boys. It would probably have led to a lot of fights later on.

The dancing platform was outdoors; that night boats arrived with a great crowd. The fiddler scraped away, dancers hooted and yelled, lovers sauntered amongst the shrubs and rocks as a big full moon came up out of the ocean throwing a gossamer veil of mystery over the whole scene. Towards eleven o'clock there being no signs of trouble, Tom took the bootlegger in his car to have him locked up in Canso, then we carefully felt our way back to the main road. It was an unusual and weird experience made laughable next morning when the trial was held before an old magistrate, stone deaf, who used a huge ear trumpet when listening to the evidence.

CHAPTER VII

A Touch of Glamour

One day when I was scouting around in my car I caught sight of my old friend A.J. Bannerman tripping along in his usual sprightly manner. I called to him but he had a worried air and I had to call again . . . asking him to "jump in and and tell me your troubles while we drive over Fraser's Mountain". There is a grand view from the top of this Cobequid hill where Prince Edward Island, Pictou Island and all those green patches of land that are scattered in Merigomish Harbour seem to lie at one's feet. Like the psalmist of old I have always felt that to the hills will I lift mine eyes from whence shall come mine aid.

A.J. told me of a falling lumber market, of stagnation in the overseas trade. "The Lord giveth and the Lord taketh away", said A.J. "But from all accounts in the newspapers and common gossip you are getting into a position of affluence through rum. I told you long ago that rum was one of our great industries and laid the foundation of many a Nova Scotia fortune."

"Not much affluence about it, A.J. I've got a tough hide and have learned by past experience how to fight with my wits and what's more important I've got friends. Without them one can't get far in this game. And I've got to thank you for your cheery advice. It helped to get my feet on the road to some of the good things of life."

It's seldom one hear's thanks for advice and we appreciate it. By the way, did you try to catch the Queen yet?"

"No I haven't. She doesn't retail any smuggled goods locally and I'm not going out of my way looking for trouble. I can find plenty on my own doorstep".

"There is a queer yarn going the rounds down the Gulf shore. The Queen was having a cargo landed from the mother-ship with her fleet of cars being loaded. She happened to see one of the men throw a case of scotch into the bushes for his future use so she made a pass at him and laid him out for two hours. The Queen was in breeches and she is hefty — must have been quite a sight. If I was in your shoes I would cultivate the friendship of such a romantic character."

"Nothing doing, A.J. I've never met her but to see her driving in her car she seems too bold. As I said before I am not looking for trouble."

A few days after meeting A.J. I was in the Deputy Stipendary's office awaiting his return to have some papers signed. A court was being held over some relative of the Queen's and she was attending, no doubt furnishing the legal talent for it was lawyer Vernon, famous criminal lawyer of Truro who was defending.

She saw me standing in the office and walked right in. The Queen of the smugglers was in her early forties, a big handsome woman with well developed bosom and hips accentuated by a neatly tailored suit. She walked with an air of abounding vitality and the sleek strength of a tiger. What a woman she was and what variety of life she had seen. Nurse, horsewoman, part-time movie actress and now back to the land of her birth to rule a crew of smugglers. In the meantime in her travels she had acquired a husband whom she also ruled.

"Hello Cliff, we are all in the same game so it is just as well to get acquainted when we are not enemies", and she whisked her famous smile in my direction. I was somewhat taken back at this cheery greeting. But it has been my good fortune in life to have known some attractive women and the best way to keep out of entanglements is to treat them decent whether they be high, low, good or bad.

"It is a pleasure to meet you under circumstances when we are not at dagger's point. Your ancestors and my ancestors have been in this country for over one hundred years and we find that to stay in Nova Scotia we have to go into the rum business though at different angles."

"Right you are, Cliff. Let me close the door", and her dainty foot slammed it shut. "We'll talk this thing over. Vernon is getting paid plenty to look after the case. One of my fore-fathers was Barney MacGee, — that's where Barney's river got it's name. We've had our roots in this soil for more than a century. Do you suppose I could get to first base in this country? Not on your life. I had to go to the States to get anywhere, then had to come home to look after my old father and mother. And was I going to stand around and see someone else make all the dough out of this smuggling racket? Not a chance. I was born to live and live I will."

"It can well be understood how a woman of your vibrant vitality could never be satisfied with the humdrum. Still you are taking a great chance. The Federal Government is going to crack down on this smuggling racket sooner or later and it wouldn't be nice for you to be caught. If I ever find occasion to have to do my duty, I'll go through with it."

"Oh, I'm taking that chance. We are paying plenty in high places to keep things running smooth. Meantime we are getting all the thrills that anyone could wish."

I wanted to see the talk come to a close for the town gossips who hung around the courthouse would have something to roll under their tongues telling how the Queen and the Inspector were closetted alone in the Magistrate's office. But she was hard to stop and I was glad to see the old Deputy put in his appearance. That was the only occasion during my four years term as Inspector that I ever had a long talk with the Queen but I always got a cheery, "High, Cliff", from her when we chanced to meet.

Deputy Stipendary Magistrate A.M. Fraser was an interesting character. Life had somehow defeated him judging by the world's standards. He had been town clerk but had lost that position by being made the goat for schemes of deeper crooks. The authorities had given him an old office and had him appointed Deputy Stipendary where he could make a few dollars on legal cases that were tried before him.

I liked to sidle into his old office and get him to talk about his youth. He had been a surveyor as a young man and had gone to the States to make a living. He had gone South to assist in building a railroad in Texas. He had a gang of slaves under him and had to often use the whip. When the Civil War broke out he had escaped to the North and, posing as an American citizen had voted for Abraham Lincoln. His hobby was pen scrollwork and he did a fine job for a man of eighty-seven.

CHAPTER VIII

The John C. Douglas Campaign

As the summer drew to its close another Federal election loomed. Tom took me aside one day to tell me that his boss, John C. Douglas, Attorney General had set his mind on running for the constituency of Antigonish-Guysboro. This would mean that a lot of his time would be spent in repairing fences in that riding. The board of stretegy told me that I would have to "lay off" our friends while the campaign was warming up. That was allright with me for I could devote my time to constable work and make some spare cash. But I had been seen going into Grit lawyers' offices and the strategy board didn't like that, figuring that the Grits would worm information out of me. But my only business was in connection with serving papers. However, I was sent for a two weeks holiday with all expenses paid to Sherbrooke in Guysboro County to keep out of harm's way and assist in the election of John C. Douglas.

During those two weeks I got an insight into the seemingly impossible accomplishments of a dynamic leader of men. It was an experience that aroused my curiosity to find out what force drove men to perform feats of resource and political valor that in ordinary course of life they would seldom or never perform.

Sherbrooke is a pretty village near the mouth of the St. Mary's one of the largest Nova Scotia rivers. It is built on a pleasant intervale at the foot of those barren rockybound hills that dot the south coast of the province. In the salmon-fishing season it is a Mecca for sportsmen. When I was there it was the nerve center of the St. Mary's municipality campaign to send John C. Douglas to Ottawa. First thing to strike me was that all the political workers were from Cape Breton. I was the only one from the mainland. Later I learned that the same held true all over. All these men were volunteers: they followed John C. as the clans of Scotland followed their chiefs. As election day drew near they kept coming and coming until John C. had to send word to Glace Bay that no more were needed. But they came, sleeping in their cars and barns just to be on hand election day to fight for John C. Losing the right to vote in their own constituency counted for nothing, party politics meant very little, what greatly mattered to them was that their chief might need help.

I have been through stormy campaigns when tempers ran high but never have I seen such loyalty to any man or to any cause as was shown by those Cape Bretoners. It seemed out of place in the twentieth century, belonging to the age of Prince Charlie, Flora MacDonald and Culloden Moor.

Hughie Dan MacLean the Warden of Cape Breton county was the spark plug and commander in chief at Sherbrooke. There was five of us under him of whom only one do I remember by name. He was John D. MacIntyre a lawyer who had been wounded overseas. Meetings had been arranged throughout the little coves and hamlets along the coast so MacIntyre took me along in the old Ford that was placed at our disposal. Finding out that I could do some speaking in a crude way he put me down as first speaker, the "burnt offering" as I was called. Then he would go at it for the effort of the evening. Sometimes Hughie Dan came along when there was any special job of fixing to be done. It was grand September weather though the nights were chilly as the fog rolled in from the Atlantic. The roads were abominable and only a Model T could have stood it.

One Grand afternoon we started for a meeting at Fisherman's Harbor. There was a ship loading pulpwood at a wharf down the river from the village. A Russian Emigree was putting through the contract and he and MacIntyre got to talking. My sparring partner went on board and came back with a quart of Bicardi Rum. That stuff had a kick like a mule and the natives there abouts were treated to a display of oratory such as they had never heard before or since. While coming home a heavy fog rolled in and we got helplessly lost. It was sunup next morning when we got back to the hotel.

It has always been a puzzle to understand how the voters of Guysboro ever stood for a bunch of outsiders running their election. The citizens of either Pictou or Cape Breton certainly wouldn't put up with it.

Right before election, Hughie Dan came to my bedroom, handed me twenty-five dollars and told me that next day a car would take me to Indian Harbour Lake polling-booth and that I must bring back a majority for John C.

"My God, Hughie, am I a stranger going in there alone and you expect me to bring out a majority? Are there any Tories there?"

"Very few that we know about. You'll have to make them, that's the way we do for John C. in Cape Breton. Good luck, remember that majority."

Bright and early the poll opened and I confronted the presiding officer, a magistrate, a leading Grit and big man of the district. In my six months as Inspector I had picked up some law and a lot of bluff. He wasn't going to allow me to stay inside but I shook the law book in his face and stood my ground inside the polling-booth. Two cars with drivers turned up to gather in the loose votes. Two women were in the booth to act as John C's agents. One belonged to one of the few Tory families in the district, the other had a sleek look. From her line of talk I gathered that she was a grass widow who had worked in an office in the States. But she knew all the answers and put lots of vim into that day's battle. By afternoon we had formed quite a battleline. In a contest such as that one's wits and grasp of what is going on must be on razor edge all the time. The magistrate and I had bitter words several times.

When the ballots were counted that evening John C had a majority of twenty-five. The grass widow eagerly took a drink of rum from a flask I had saved for the occasion, we danced a jig then I got into a taxi and back to Sherbrooke.

The gang were none too cheerful for a Captain Burns a Grit politician who knew his stuff had upset one district that had been counted on as sure for John C. He correctly worked on the theory that in Guysboro an election is an event when the voters can make five dollars apiece. He had his ammunition and then gave them the works. However the overall picture was that John C had been elected. So all bills having been paid we hurried to Antigonish to get the results. On that trip Hughie Dan told us about the plans the Federal Government had in mind for curbing smuggling.

Federal officers with new cars were to be appointed as a preventative service, armed speedboats were to be used along the coast and I was to get a real job out of it for the good work I had done during the campaign. But alas! what a sad story we learned when we arrived at Antigonish: John C. had been elected but the government had been defeated and now the Grits were in power at Ottawa. It was they who were to put the new preventative system into effect and hand out the good jobs that would ultimately break the smuggling racket.

One can look back at all that sound and fury of that election and cogitate on what it all amounted to. For me it had meant an unparalleled experience to show what a dynamic man can do with a well organized band of followers. For when it is considered that Antigonish-Guysboro was Catholic and had been consistently Grit, that John C was Protestant while his opponent MacIsaac was a fine Celtic gentleman and a Catholic, then can we see what leadership our candidate had in his makeup.

I can never forget the sight of him in his undershirt and trousers sitting on the edge of the bed in the Prince George Hotel greeting priests, ministers and workers of every shade and variety as they came along for a handshake and a word of cheer. It was the first and only time I ever saw him alive. He left for Halifax, cleaned up his affairs as Attorney General and went to Ottawa. There were bitter recriminations about his election principally from his own party. Death overtook him in Montreal the following winter and his body was brought to New Glasgow for burial as he was a native son.

The day of the funeral was bitter February weather but his followers came by the dozen for the distance of one hundred and seventy-five miles to pay their last respects to their chief. No king or potentate could have a finer tribute at their grave than the tears shed by those hardboiled clansmen.

Nova Scotia needs men like John C. Douglas if they could be persuaded to work and fight for the good of their native province.

Chapter IX

Some In-Fighting

In Pictou County the election had been fought in peaceable gentlemanly fashion between Tory Colonel Cantley and Grit James A. Fraser editor of the Eastern Chronicle. They were personal friends and relatives and the fact that the liquor inspctor had been taken out of the district had not leaked out until after election. James A. had been defeated and when that trick had been brought to his attention the next issue of the Eastern Chronicle made all our faces red. James A. Fraser could write.

Several of the bootleggers cleaned up in good style during the "holiday" and they were now ready for a campaign of raids and fines. The council again raised my salary and very foolishly I began to be puffed up.

During my period in office I had got several anonymous letters the import of which was to tell where rum could be found. I had tried several times to catch Clarence MacDermid, had searched his home, found numerous clever "hides", but could not get his rum. At that time he had working for him one Bill Robinson. Robinson's mother was a good old lady belonging to the Salvation Army. Amongst the numerous anonymous letters received was one giving in detail the hiding place in Robinson's home of MacDermid's rum.

It was written from the standpoint of someone who had a spite at MacDermid and seemed genuine. So armed with a search-warrant we ran-sacked the premises. Of course I didn't get any rum and felt heartily ashamed of myself and lost friends by being so stupid as to give heed to a letter of that nature.

Amongst the many institutions of New Glasgow's Front Street where topics of the hour were held under the searchlight of wisdom was Colonel Bob Murray's barber shop. And the greatest talker was Charlie Lorimer, a barber. It had come to my ears that Charlie was doing a lot of tongue-wagging about the Inspector's graft. One day we had to arrest him and he had on his person a bottle of rum. The N.S.T.A. provided a hundred dollar fine for that offence. I didn't want to see him soaked but the idea struck me that as J. Stanley Fraser, an enthusiastic young Tory, had just opened a law office it would be a good chance to give him his first case.

Stan had a couple of chairs, an old desk and was trying to fix an old typewritter when I walked in. He and I had grown up together and I knew that he had in him a smart streak. He was an offhanded chap a friend to everyone and bright in the knowhow of politics.

"Want to get your first case in court, Stan?"

"Yes, but not to prosecute for you."

"This is not for me but against me. I've got Charlie Lorimer locked up for 'illegal possession' and it might not require much legal talent to get him clear. If you could do that, well you would know how the gossip would fly in the barber shop. Your name would be up in lights."

"O.K. Cliff, what time in court?"

"Ten o'clock. You've got twenty minutes to get his story."

Stan defended Lorimer and got him clear. Soon his fame bounded to the skies. The Tories didn't have a lawyer with a proper slant on the under-world to chisel in and get their permanent support. Dannie MacLennan, shrewd old fox, soon had Stan in a bright office in a building that he owned on Front Street. Also gleaming oak furniture and a pretty stenograpHer. So Stan began to go places.

The high and low were always welcome in his office. He threw all his energy into winning cases that could possibly be of any benefit to the Conservative Party. He gathered around him a doubtful clientele that gave him prestige with the bootlegging fraternity as he continued to win cases. The smugglers and the retailers with their friends and families formed a large proportion of the population. Thus Stan's influence on political trends was considerable.

When Christmas came around he didn't forget his old friends, for I received a handsome gold watch from him. Yes, he was going up like a rocket. Many years afterwards I found out how he got that watch: he had gone down to Dannie and had persuaded his landlord to give him the price of the watch "as a gift for the Inspector".

To be liquor Inspector at Christmas was to be an artful dodger. The old hands at police work impressed on me that this was the season of "peace on earth and goodwill towards bootleggers". So before the holiday season there was very little raiding carried on. Christmas eve was a happy one at the police station. I had four turkeys given me and it was the merriest one at my home that I ever experienced. The wife and children all had a wonderful time. So I thought in my heart, "Great is the mellowing power of rum".

That Christmas day I went up the mountain to see my mother and father who were still alive and take some presents as I had always done.

They were glad to see me. My father was especially eager to hear about the smugglers. But he was solemn on this occasion. The stories carried by the press of the raids and court trials of that prohibition era disturbed him. He was over eighty but could still grasp the significance of events. It was comforting to see that good care was given them by my sister.

"I'm thinking that the devil is abroad in the world seeing whom he may destroy", my father said with great solemnity. "Why do people go into the hateful busniess of selling rum?"

"From different motives, principally to make a living. Other means of survival are dying out while in the rum game they can get something to eat, have a few of the comforts of life and sociability."

"And what about the damnation to their souls for living by these unholy means?"

"People don't fuss much nowadays about their souls if they can fill their bellies. The world even in Presbyterian Pictou has thrown away many of the old time principles of right and wrong."

I didn't tell him that his remarks had disturbed my conscience. To my parent's way of thinking, working at the carpenter trade was an honorable way to make a living. Alternately they were happy when newspaper headlines told of a spectacular raid I had been in or dubious at my new life so thrilling and prosperous.

"Of what shall it profit a man if he gain the whole world and lose his soul. The Lord hath laid it down in His Book for the children of Israel and for us all from everlasting until everlasting. Except the people repent of their sins and come humbly before Him they shall be destroyed, utterly, all the great cities of the world. He has given to us in North America the best continent on this earth and what has been done with it? Babylon in all its glory and wickedness was not half so great. Except they repent of their sins they shall be destroyed."

To this I could make no answer. My parents belonged to a fading age of faith and another way of life had been forced by circumstances upon [me].

A few weeks later my mother died. Pneumonia had caught her frail body and never again would her children or grandchildren get her warmhearted smile after we had climbed the mountain to the old homestead. I can still see her rocking and knitting as she hummed the old Scotch psalm, —

> "The man who once hath found abode
> Within the sacred place of God,
> Shall with Almighty God abide,
> And in his shadow safely hide."

The onrush of Greed speeded up by the invention of the gasoline engine have wiped out her way of life as effectively as Rome had destroyed Carthage.

CHAPTER X

Incidents of the Battlefield

During winter months the Trade was not raided as ruthlessly as had been the case in the summer months. The "wholesalers" had their supplies carefully hidden and found little difficulty in the early morning hours of landing gallon cans of rum to their retailers. However, sometimes at these joints some criminal action would occur that would call for a severe raid.

Sometime in the month of March, 1927, I took part in one of the worst raids of my four years in the Trade. It took place in Westville and was conducted by Tom MacKay. Andrew MacNeil was running a joint above a store on Main Street and the town authorities were stumped to put him out of business because Andrew had a lot of friends and relatives. Matt Richardson, manager of the Drummond colliery was a member of the town council and being a man who would have his own way, wanted to smash Andrew. To make matters worse "Black Tom", Andrew's father and Matt were always at loggerheads in the mine. "Black Tom" was rugged, a man to be reckoned with and he loved to defy his boss. Bill Roy, one of the gamest cops I have ever worked with, had been appointed Inspector as well as being chief-of-police. However the council decided that putting Andrew out of business was asking too much of the chief.

So they called in the aid of Tom McKay. He asked me to go along as it would likely be quite an affair. Sometimes miners will fight against themselves but it is to bad for an outsider to interfere.

Tom thought it advisable for Matt to come along as well as another councillor, Mr. Henderson by name. It was snowing that night and the slush was deep. We hid behind a board fence across the street and could see customers being let in and out through the street door. It was Saturday night, paynight.

If Matt Richardson had had his way that shop would have been blown up. Tom MacKay, having a lot of experience was cautious on a raid. The plan was for the Chief, Tom and I to rush the stairs after some customer got in and the councillors to stay outside and watch affairs. In those days I could be fast on my feet and the chief was one of the best boxers in Nova Scotia. So when the opportunity came we rushed the door but there was a nightlatch on the inside. I didn't hesitate to smash the glass and open it.

We went up the stairs on the bound, just in time to see Andrew throw a can of rum out through the window. There was a washtub on the floor full of beer on ice. I threw myself on top of it as Black Tom tried to pick it up to heave it outside. He made a pass at me but the chief caught him by the arm and neck. Andrew's wife grabbed the kettle of hot water from the stove but Tom yelled for them to stop or be arrested for starting a riot. It was hot while it lasted but we got the beer. The rum that had been thrown out through the window had been grabbed by a young chap. Matt Richardson caught him and he was fined one hundred dollars for illegal possession.

That Trial in Westville was a big one. The courthouse was packed. The magistrate had just been appointed by the Tories and as Westville was a Tory town it made things hard for him. I've forgotten how it ended as it was adjourned and dragged on. Anyhow, Matt Richardson got disgusted with prohibition enforcement and didn't go on any more raids.

Black Tom or Andrew and I still have a great laugh over that fight when we meet.

One of the worst dives in New Glasgow was run by Mrs. Billie N.. Her husband was a war casualty and was capable of anything while drunk. Delores was her name. A mite of a woman savage and cruel. Her obscene and profane tongue was feared by friend and foe and she was smart at selling rum and hard to catch. Many, many times had she cut her hands on broken rum bottles as she smashed them in the sink while we hammered down her doors. Her sink, like that of all retail bootleggers, had no trap to catch the rum. She hated cops and cheerfully told us so in her lurid language.

A girl of sixteen belonging to honest hardworking parents had got into the habit of frequenting this dive. They had tried all their powers of persuasion to prevent her but still she would go. Her father had gone to J.W.H. Sutherland, editor of the Evening News, with his plea to have something done. Mr. Sutherland was a progressive citizen, a square-shooter and a good Tory. On several occasions he had steered my course into smooth-running channels. He told me that he would "lay off" for a couple of days to see what I could do to clean up the situation. So a special raid was planned. A raid that came within an ace of being my last.

We carried it out in an early hour of a Sunday morning in March. The house was built above the railroad embankment and was open on all sides. Four of us crawled over the embankment, listening for sounds that would denote carelessness as Delores opened the door to new customers. A thick heavy fog had rolled in before we wormed ourselves into position behind the rude shelter built around the business entrance. I cautioned the boys to protect the sink and rum pitcher and to spare no one come what may.

As two half-drunken customers were admitted we rushed the joint. I made for the sink and so did Delores. The rum was in a pint bottle that she grabbed to smash. By good luck I grabbed her wrist and caught the bottle with my other hand. I had not seen her husband pick up a beer bottle and slip up behind me. He swung but the blow was deflected by officer Langille catching him around the neck. As it was the bottle hit the back of my head, had I not been wearing a heavy winter cap I would not be hammering out these lines today. Some customers started to put up a fight but were thrown in a corner. Officer McCann got hold of the broken neck of the beer bottle and it makes a nasty weapon at any time.

Delores was fined in court. The Evening News played up the trial and the dangers officers met in the town dives. Privately I told Delores that she must stay put of business for three months or we would "camp on her doorstep" and put her out of business. This "camp on your doorstep" was a sentence that no bootlegger wanted.

"How the flameing H--- do you expect me to get enough to eat for three months if I can't sell rum" asked Delores.

"I don't know and I don't care. You've gone to far having girls around your joint. From now on it's do as we say or else...."

She burned the air with colorful oaths but I had a thick hide in those days. I knew that she would still sell rum for she liked depraved companionship. Also, I knew that she had bought her house from one of the town councillors with time payments.

CHAPTER XI

The End of the Beginning

When a year of Inspectorship had rolled around I took stock of circumstances. I had collected thousands of dollars in revenue for the town, some bad characters had been sent to jail, the bootleggers had tightened up their system, but otherwise there was as much rum sold as ever. As for myself I had acquired a degree of prosperity that a brief year before would seem impossible. I was learning to live and laugh. Along with these things a sense of mental sharpness in the pursuit of my duties had grown upon me. I could sense friends or enemies and forsee dangerous situations. This sixth sense along with Dannie MacLennan's caution, "to survive we must be able to change with changing conditions", made me mentally alert in all matters of law. Surprisingly enough I found the biggest danger I had to face was the chance of getting a "swelled head". The flattery of the limelight is always a dangerous thing.

Having spare time on my hands the thought of polishing up my crude knowledge of English began to assert itself. Bought some technical books, paper pencils and a typewriter and labouriously tried to write short stories. But they wouldn't click. However it wasn't time wasted for years later when I got into the tourist business the knowledge of composition did me good service.

Often did I speculate on the infiltration of the Rum Trade. The bootleggers were great buyers of new cars. They spent their money lavishly on new clothes. Even the business of selling rum cans was a noticeable item in the trade of a well-established hardware firm. Also, I began to learn that there were powerful forces near the top in politics who were holding off the day when a preventative force to curb smuggling would be set up. In the body politic it was hard to tell who didn't have a finger in the pie.

A watchful eye had been kept on Delores and before three months were up I felt that her trade was becoming too open. One fine summer day in June while passing in my car I saw a window of her house open and without a flyscreen. Stopping the car I told Officer Langille to follow me. Diving through I rushed for the sink. But she was too quick for me. She smashed the bottle and gave herself a bad cut. An old timer of the town, "Posty Chisholm", had a partly filled glass of rum in front of him. This was taken and I asked "Posty" Did you find this to be rum you were drinking?

"Never saw it till you pointed it out to me."

"Posty, you can tell that one to the judge."

"Sure thing, Cliff, sure thing at any time."

For wit and dramatic situations that was a notable trial. Stan Fraser was her lawyer and the fireworks between he and I were interesting. We put "Posty" on the stand as our witness. Rod G. was my lawyer as usual.

"What were you doing in Delores N--------'s house on the afternoon of June 7th?"

"I was looking for buyers for a line of books."

"What books?"

"Pilgrim's Progress, for one."

"Did you have any rum to drink in that house on the afternoon of June 7th?"

"No, didn't know she sold rum."

"Do you understand the nature of an oath?"

"Sure thing, I do."

"Do you believe in God?"

"Lookahere Rod G, I'll have you know that I'm a better Presbyterian than you are."

Stan went ahead with the cross-examination.

"This liquid that was on the table beside you, was it rum?"

"I'm sure I don't know."

"If your honor pleases, the Inspector says it is rum, yet his own witness with an extensive knowledge of life says under oath that he knew of no rum being there. I submit, your honor, that I be permitted to sample this presumed rum."

"You may do that."

Stan tilted the glass and drank the evidence.

When Delores got on the stand in her own defence and was asked her name, she answered, "Delores N--------, ninety-eight pounds of Hell."

"No, no she never sold rum within the space of three months." Such perjury would be hard to beat and I lost the case.

With such victories and close attention to politics Stan Fraser was acquiring a provincial reputation as a constructive organizer. Across Canada R.B. Bennett was making passes to jump into the Premiership, so an organizer was wanted in Nova Scotia who could put pep into the party and Stan was picked for the job. As I remember it he was supposed to get five thousand dollars per year and expenses. Not bad picking for less than a year from the time he had got Charlie Lorimer free.

We had a great fishing trip to Archibald's lake that spring, only marred by one incident. Early one morning after the boys had had a bit of a spree, I fortunately had hidden the rum some distance from the cabin. On these occasions it was but little liquor I drank except a "slug" when travelling from one part of the lake to another.

We were awakened by wild whoops coming through the woods. Soon Black Tom MacNeil and some Westville miners appeared on the scene. The boys had no stomach to come out of the cabin to see Tom looking under every bush for the Inspector's rum. I was left to "kid" them along and they didn't find our ammunition.

The Town council had again raised my salary and being all good Tories were up to that time just one big happy family. I was rolling a lot of solid cash into the town treasury and even James A. Fraser of Eastern Chronicle fame had little criticism.

Towards the middle of June Tom MacKay informed us that he was going to make a big haul in Guysboro County. Five of us went down with him on that raid. That county at that time was a smuggler's paradise. Its lonely harbours and isolated hamlets with few custom's officers made it easy for the Trade.

I have forgotten the exact location of the ambush but it was somewhere out of Boyleston. We waited until early morning hours when three cars heavily loaded with rum kegs rolled into the yard of a deserted farm. It was bitterly cold for that time of year and I took to shivering. Never being tough or rugged physically I knew that I had caught a severe cold. The early rays of the sun felt good to us all and especially to me. It was a great haul of rum that had belonged to a Grit smuggler from Halifax. The events of the day are not clear to me except that the custom's officer in Guysboro town didn't want to have anything to do with the catch.

When I got home I had to go to bed but was around in a few days making preperations for a trip with the wife and family and some friends to Cape Breton. So on the day after the trial in Guysboro town we continued on to that royal island.

The weather was hot and to me it eased a trip of misery, for I was sick, more sick than I realized. The glories of Margaree, Lake Ainslee, Bein Breagh and Nyanza I saw through a fog of fever. In Sydney the Isle Royal Hotel was in the course of construction, the Governor General was visiting the city so we had to put up at some second-class affair that I can only remember for its shabbiness and smells.

As soon as I got home I was packed away to bed and the doctor said "pleurisy". A treacherous evil of a disease being closely related to tuberculosis. I suffered a lot but had a charming and efficient nurse. This along with the visitations of a host of friends during those lovely summer days made the time pass quickly. This incident of sickness would be immaterial to this story were it not that in my absence the seeds were sown for future storms and perils in the Trade. During the early days of August when in the silly manner of convalescents I began to enquire of my nurse, her telephone number, place of residence, etc., she told me that her days of vigil were over. So I began to move around in my car.

Fred Milligan took me aside and told me that his principal yard worker, Paddy Nolan, famous hockey player of the Maritime circuit couldn't get a job. So the strategy committee had agreed to allow him to open a soft drink shop on "Back" Street where he could sell the odd glass of something stronger. It didn't sound so good to me but Paddy was a likeable fellow and I felt that he would do as he was told. I was still under doctor's care and didn't want to take on any fights. I wanted to hold my job, I wanted to stay alive. So it became my conviction that there must be no more raiding trips involving night-work and bad weather. I must stay in my own baliwick, or be prepared to go a sanitorium.

Looking backward, it is wonderful that I ever survived that decision. It amounted to the fact that henceforth I must put my wits against some powerful former friends, a diseased body and the subtle cunning of the liquor interests.

Walter Weir had gone out of the town council and George Grant had been elected in his place. With George the success of the Conservative party was of first importance for the game was everything. He was a good politician and political intrigue was right up his alley.

Undercover, Fred Milligan was securing the land for the press town parking lot, and was doing a good job for the citizens with the growth of motor traffic. New Glasgow was fast becoming a shopping centre. It is imperative to remember that in those Roaring Twenties we all belived that nothing could stop our soap-bubble prosperity. Anyhow, someone on the inside conceived the idea that the streets close by the parking lot would become valuable property. Fred was quietly picking up some property but one day he found out that Walter Weir and Tom MacKay had bought a lot with an old barn on it that he had been trying to acquire. He lost his temper for he saw that somone had "squealed".

This incident led to such bitterness and emotion that as the years rolled on the well geared Tory machine of those days was ultimately cracked. For me, however, it was a chance for me to get away from liquor raids outside the town. In other words, through sickness I had begun to grow old.

Fred as chairman of police issued orders that there was to be no fraternizing with Tom MacKay or outside inspectors. And he sought by political power to prevent outside inspectors from raiding in New Glasgow. George Grant with his usual political astuteness tried to prevent the quarrel from breaking into the open.

Jim Caldwell had been made chief-of-police some time before and he and Tom MacKay were old friends. But Fred issued orders to him also. No friendship with Tom MacKay or else . . . . The happy political family of former years was through, the honeymoon was over. Through this submerged tempest the Paddy Nolan case became the scandal of the town. Paddy had been Fred's right-hand man in elections, and now he boldly went to the M.P.'s and told them that no political inspector dare touch Paddy Nolan. Paddy, being Irish and human felt puffed up by such sweeping protection and sold rum quite openly in the heart of the town. The temperance forces spurred on by the Grits who had an inkling of the quarrel, were loud in their denunciation of this flagrant rum selling. So it was a "hot seat" that I had to sit upon.

Taking stock of the situation and knowing the craftiness of Tom in liquor prosecution and intrigue, I resolved wherever possible to cut down and centre all liquor raids and prosecutions to those conducted with Sergeant Langille. Thus we continued as fast friends to hunt, fight and "cover up" together as long as prohibition lasted. We both became nimble-witted and learned to know all the "rat holes" of escape. Together we carried out Dannie MacLennan's injunction, — "to survive we must learn to change with changing conditions".

Sometimes it was puzzle to know what course to pursue with the conflicting tides of power. About this time the Liberals at Ottawa started their long-heralded preventative force for smuggling along the coast had become a national scandal. Norman MacDonald, chief-of-police at Trenton and Major Warren Jollimore were provided with cars writs of assistance and told to go to it and stop the smuggling. Fred could not get any protection for Paddy from this quarter but Paddy was cagey and continued to do business at the old stand.

One dark night when beset with this web of intrigue, I went down to see Dannie to get his view of the tangled situation, knowing him to be clear-headed and having the craft of a Jesuit.

He was surprised and pleased to see me. For my part I was afraid but determined to get his angle. He ushered me into his private office, pulled a box of excellent cigars and we had a rare evening together. There I learned more about the inner workings of the Trade than I had learned in all my previous experience. Dannie was a great host and an excellent talker.

We discussed local politics and the boom on the stock market. Then I said, "Dannie, have you heard anything about a row amongst local politicians and prominent Tories"?

"You mean between our chairman of police and some liquor Inspector?"

"That's it." The kingpin of the Trade in Eastern Nova Scotia evidently had a good grapevine.

"It isn't a good thing for any of us. I wouldn't want such open protection as Paddy Nolan is getting. That is asking for continual raids from the

Grits new preventative force. Fred doesn't understand this rum game and being a determined man may be like a bull in a chinashop. I wouldn't want to be in your shoes."

"If I had my health again I would enjoy the thrill of matching wits with those opposing forces. But things being what they are I believe I'll have to play down my position in the game."

"That would seem to be your best bet. You've had your share of the limelight. Some Inspectors crave that stuff all the time — but in the payoff there is nothing to it. Friends are your greatest asset, someone you can go to when you are in a tight spot. Things are booming just now with the building of the Guysboro railroad. New Glasgow will be the centre to which the crews will gravitate for their payday celebrations so there will be some loose change around for all concerned. The stockmarket is also booming and cars will be pushing each other on the street. So try to get Fred to pipe down and not to upset the gravy."

"I had something like that in mind, Dannie. What is your opinion of this stockmarket boom?"

"Have you any money in it, Cliff?"

"No, I haven't. But to see them opening fancy offices with all the contraptions of a stockmarket makes one wonder what is behind it, that's all."

"If you haven't got anything in it, keep out of it, because I know you can't afford to lose. I have friends who tip me off now and then and I make the odd dollar. But I play it for the kick that's in it. It is no game for a poor man to indulge in. A lot of the boys will lose their shirts sooner or later. A continent-wide prosperity is rolling along now but government extravagance and the huge public debt is more than can be kept going. It is bound to collapse unless there is another war. That would keep the old chariot going. It is a strange thing how democracy can organize for war but go broke forming the ways and means of peace."

"In other words, we should do as the bees and squirrels do, put something by for a rainy day."

"Exactly Clifford. It will likely be a long, long spell without sun."

Looking backward, Dannie MacLennan's insight into human nature and his correct summary of events are to me a marvel. How different was an hour's talk with him than was the drivel dispensed by so-called leaders of public opinion! Yet to the Holy Willies he was a sinner above all others. Often have I put in hours of mental gymnastics trying to add up the factors that experience and belief had taught me, yet to get an answer that would stand up, I could not. Many a time while on a trip doing police work I would park my car near some beauty spot with which Eastern Nova Scotia abounds and try to reason out these contradictions.

In the fall of 1927 my father died. With his death was severed a last link with boyhood dreams and the memories of the good old days before World War I. He could tell great stories of the romance attached to the ship-building days in Pictou County. He trusted in his God, he loved his native land and though a poor farmer he had finer thoughts than meat-and-potatoes. He looked askance at my seeming prosperity and the hard-boiled manner and ways that had grown upon me.

Early in December two detectives from Inspector Grant's provincial department swooped down on the town, bought liquor in several of our local dives and a furore was created in the Trade. I was tipped off early in the "putch" so Sergeant Langille and I pulled several raids, got the rum and brought the cases to court the same day as the detectives had set down theirs. I had previous knowledge of several bootlegger's hides along with their method of selling and had saved the knowledge for such a time as this.

Chief Inspector Grant, a lawyer, personally conducted the detective's cases. Rod G was my lawyer as always with my victims pleading "guilty". That was a field day in the court house. J. Stanley Fraser defended all the liquor cases and being then at the peak of his power he made a brave showing. As I remember it the detectives didn't win a case. Rod G made the sage remark at the end of the trials, "that will learn those superior-minded Haligonians not to poach on our preserves".

Christmas again came around with its festivities and shower of turkeys. With my New Year's report showing over seven thousand dollars collected in fines the town council were very well pleased. I had learned to sense public reactions and timed raids and splurges so as to stop the clamor.

In those days most of us put up our cars in the winter on account of the snow not being removed from the streets. So our duties were carried out on foot. This lessened the sudden surprise but money was abundant and we got plenty convictions.

Having lots of time on my hands I tried my best to write something that would be accepted for publication but it was "no dice".

[From here was deleted the description of a six week visit to the Southern United States beginning in March, 1928 as Rose sought to recover his health.]

CHAPTER XII
Holding Our Own

My family was surprised and glad to see me. It was almost midnight when I got home but I called up some of my "stools" and found out some disturbing news. Our system of control had largely been taken over by the forces opposed to Fred Milligan and I saw that I was due for an upset unless I acted quickly. So I took my car and hustled down street, got the "lowdown" and went after the bootleggers and got two convictions before two o'clock A.M. I also got a hot tip that a load of beer was to be delivered from the freightshed next morning. So again getting into my car after shutting my garage doors as a blind I secured a good hiding place in Grant's lumberyard opposite the freightshed.

Sure enough when the doors rolled open Charlie Forbes with his chestnut horse and sloven backed in and loaded seven barrels of beer. As soon as he was well on his way I jumped him. Oh, it was a grand feeling to know that my luck still held! These surprise raids made quite a stir around town and the newspapers were full of it. Nothing could compare with the old strategy of "audacity, audacity and more audacity". The control of the local Trade, as far as I wanted it was safe.

It was great to feel the thrill of being healthy again. Police work aplenty came my way from the lawyers. The use of my car made money for me, more money than I ever dreamed was to be had in chasing crime. Cash was plentiful and as I had learned to talk the same language as the lawyers we would discuss the merits of different cases and they put several good things my way.

As for the liquor prosecution, I had turned it into a licence system. The town fathers were pleased to get the revenue so we slipped along quite smoothly. There were few incidents worthy of recording that summer but two still stand out in my memory.

A local bootlegger tipped me that an outside smuggler from Moncton, N.B., was to take in two carloads of rum and whiskey. Concealing my car in a woodroad branching off the main highway, Sergeant Langille and I waited until a coupe answering the description given me rolled along. Then we set chase. A foolish stunt and the joke was on me for coming around a turn he passed another car and in attempting to get around the obstructing car I got ditched and smashed my carwheel. Later I was told that the car I was chasing was loaded with stone, it being the "blind", the car with the rum following and cutting off went to Stellarton. This fiasco got into the newspapers with the result that I got the "raspberry" from the wise guys along the Front Street. I resolved that never again would I chase a rum caravan.

Another event of that summer that stands out was a picnic, three carloads of our friends with visitors from the States, had one fine Sunday afternoon in July at Cape George lighthouse.

About two miles offshore was a rumrunning schooner, her spars gleaming in the hot summer sun. Cape George is a high noble promintery with the light on top of a cliff about five hundred [feet] above the sea. As we got out of the car, who did I see coming around the lighthouse but a wellknown smuggler with fieldglasses and a flag under his arm. He actually got sick when he saw me and laid himself down in the shadow of the light until we had our lunch and had gone. I wasn't chasing smugglers that day but was having fun with my family and friends.

On the south side of the Cape a road is cut out of the cliff and winds down to Balantyne's Cove where there is a wharf, store and a few houses. [At] that time the road was a rough wheeltrack, steep and dangerous. Legend has it that the Queen of smugglers would go down that road at night in her big Buick without lights. Balantyne's Cove was an ideal spot to land rum.

The storekeeper was a Mr. MacEachern whom I had been told was as learned in Highland lore as a dominee from Aberdeen. He was in his store that day his face flushed and tongue thick with the Gaelic and good smuggled Scotch as he dispensed bits of history or battle murder and sudden death by loch and darkened glen. Amongst our company was Sam Campbell, wellknown baker and business man of New Glasgow.

I got MacEachern talking about the exploits of Bonnie Prince Charlie. Said he to me, "An' what might your name be?"

"MacGregor, a good Highland name". It was the name of one of my grandmothers.

"Oog, 'twas bonnie fighters were the MacGregors, They were oot with Prince Charlie. And' what might this gentleman's name be", turning to Sam Campbell.

"Campbell, another good Scotch name".

The storekeeper's face swelled up as though it would burst. "Get all oot o' my store. The Deil the Campbell will drink in my store this day. Betrayed the MacDonalds at Glencoe an' ye were na' oot wi' the Prince. So get oot". Strange that battles two centuries old should becloud a picnic thousands of miles away.

That year slipped pleasantly away with few spectacular raids. The provincial election was held with the Conservatives going back with a greatly reduced majority. This loss can be attributed to stupidity on the part of politicians. Their appointed officials not being used to the reins of power made some terrible blunders. The Liberals were elated and were coming out bleating their smug assumption that the power and the glory in Nova Scotia belonged to them.

That autumn I bought a lot of land and went ahead to build a modern bungalow to occupy my time and use up any spare cash. The countrywide craze playing the stockmarket was in full swing. Three bucket shops were opened on Front Street and did a land office business. Even if I was a chestnut joke to the "wise guys" it seemed safer to have real estate than a stock certificate.

At that time there was a joint operated on MacDonald street by a frowsy lady and numerous complaints had come to the police about workers on the Guysboro railroad being rolled when being in there with some girl. Sergeant Langille, being a clean man, didn't like to pull a raid there for the danger of catching syphilis could not be overlooked. Search as we might we could not find her "hide". One day in Westville I saw one of the girls that frequented her dive and feeling that I might get some information, I asked if she wanted a drive to town. She said she did. I put the questions to her, pointed out that it would be to her advantage to tell me where her frowsy-headed matron kept her rum. She came through with the information that it was hid on a shelf underneath the kitchen table. It was so simple that we never thought of looking there.

One paynight in December we raided the dive and found three bottles of rum. The case was brought to court, she fought it but was convicted. She told me she would have to go to jail, no fooling. She started to get her clothes together when I said, "Anne, I don't feel like putting you in jail Christmas eve, so I'll give you three days to find the cash".

That Christmas many a nice present came my way but none made me feel that I was still a human being more than a dainty expensive silk muffler from the frowsy lady, with a card, "Thanks for letting me stay out over Xmas". However three days after Christmas when she had sobered up I took her to the County jail.

The year 1928 ended with the best financial returns from rum that I had ever earned for the Town. Over ten thousand dollars from fines. The city fathers were well pleased.

CHAPTER XIII

Of Withered Pastures

The Federal Government had named A.T. Logan as chief preventative officer for the province. A giant of a man with great physical endurance and courage. He meant business. He shook the smuggling racket as a great wind shakes an orchard. One Pictou County smuggler lost over two thousand gallons of rum.

This cross raiding by different batches of prosecutors made the Trade expensive and hazardous. During 1929 the fines were much more difficult to collect.

Liquor "Hides" were becoming more ingenious and hard to locate.

Some of these pieces of ingenuity are worthy of mention. Sometines we found them by luck, close observation, or a tipoff. A bootlegger should never drink liquor. It arouses his braggadocio and loosens his tongue. He wants to show his friends how he fools the police. These same friends in a moment of spite will soon betray him.

False thresholds, false steps, secret panels are old stuff. One of [the] safest was for one of the "Mothers" to carry several bottles attached to [her] waist under a billowy shirt.

In one dive I knocked out the leg of a stove, shifted the floor protector and found two gallons of rum.

Beer being a bulky article was hard to conceal. But one bootlegger had us fooled. He put up a partition of secondhand sheathing in his cellar and worked the bolts on the inner side of the door with magnets. But he got drunk and showed it to false friends.

Another system was to get an ingenious plumber to manipulate the water pipes and keep the rum in a hidden tank.

But to my knowledge the best and one that was never found out was explained to me years afterwards by the owner when he had gone into a lawful successful business. He had a deep hole dug in his cellar, buried a hundred gallon mollasses cask with an inch pipe long enough to come to the top of the concrete floor. Then the whole thing was cemented over except the pipe, the cask was filled with rum, a cork inserted in the pipe, then coal was shovelled over the whole affair. When rum was wanted a plumbob was dropped from a nail driven directly above the pipe, the cork was pulled and a pump put down.

During 1929 the agitation started for Government control and the Harrington Government at Halifax promised a referendum on the matter. Constable work was brisk and I often more than doubled my salary from this source. In this line of work there were many experiences from the seamy side of life, the rough side of the lath and plaster.

The most touching sight I've ever seen took place on the steps of the Nova Scotia Hospital for the insane in Dartmouth. Some forgotten committeeman with an eye for landscape beauty had picked that location. It has a sweep of grandeur that can't be surpassed. It was often my duty to take patients to that institution and one gets hardened to that terrible affliction of insanity.

The case in point was that of Mr. Fraser a farmer of forty-five years who in the middle of winter had gone insane from living alone. He was a big man of fine appearance and in conversation showed some appreciation of the finer things of life. It was a cold clear day in February, a feathery fall of snow undisturbed by wind glistened like a million diamonds on the gaunt hardwoods and evergreens.

As we went up the wide circular steps at the public entrance, he turned and said, "Mr. Rose, could I stand here for a little while before I am taken inside?"

"Sure", I said.

At the top step he turned, took off his heavy winter cap and gazed across Halifax Harbour to where the city climbs the slopes of Citadel Hill. Then the tears began to fall as he murmured, "Goodbye trees, goodbye blue sky, Goodbye God, goodbye everything. Take me inside, Mr. Rose".

The worst legal work I was ever called upon to do was to kidnap a little girl from school. It was all perfectly legal. Somewhere in the Lorne district, in the heart of Presbyterian Pictou County, three girls had been left as orphans in the early teens. The two older ones soon became the sport of man's lust and when I knew them they ran a bugbeer joint on Frederick Street in New Glasgow. The youngest girl had been taken into a good home in New Lairg.

As I remember it there lived in this home two brothers, one of them married. These brothers had a sister married to a wealthy man in California. This sister and her husband had come home for a visit and the American had got the idea of adopting and educating the child who was now about twelve. He went to Cape Breton to get the adoption papers.

Someone put him onto my trail so I was given the task of getting the child. The whole transaction had a dirty smell and I had no alibis. I waited in my car behind some trees near the New Lairg school until recess. Then I approached the children and asked them about the girl. She came over and I told her that friends were waiting to see her in New Glasgow before they left for the States. She asked me if she could get her schoolbag. Pausing for a moment to reflect, I said , "No, you can get it when you come back". That was the last she ever saw of the New Lairg school for many a long year. In California she became educated and married a wealthy man.

But it was a miserable hour for me some days later when one of the brothers came to the police with tears in his eyes asking for his little girl.

The funniest experience to come my way while in police work occurred on a cold January day. Near the boundary of New Glasgow on the West Side there lived two sisters, one a widow with two boys and the other sister being a grass widow. One day the police station got a call from these ladies to have two dogs destroyed that the boys were having around the premises. The grass widow was a looker allright built along the gay Nineties style of beauty with generous curves in the proper places. She might have been in her late twenties, knew all the answers and from her line of talk had evidently "been around".

Not long afterwards, one frosty morning, Rev. Mr. Wilkinson the agent of the Children's Aid Society hailed me to ask, "Mr. Rose could you tell me where Mrs.---------- lives?" I liked the good old man for he was trying to do his duty with an earnest desire to benefit destitute children.

"Certainly, Mr. Wilkinson, It's quite a distance, ten below zero, so I'll drive you there."

He thanked me and got into the car. I was curious to see the reaction when he met the grass widow.

The kitchen was small and a roaring fire was in the stove. A sink, a table, three chairs and the stove filled it. Mr. Wilkinson sat near the stove with the gay lady in her dainty revealing negligee across from him. I sat near the outside door where it was cooler.

He tried to explain his errand in connection with her nephews but the heat of the stove and the lady's seductive perfume was to strong for him to make a convincing argument.

"I feel that we have introduced this grave matter concerning the boys as well as the situation will allow at the present time. I have other matters of grave import to look into at the present time. So, Mr. Rose, I feel that I must go."

I agreed with him for that kichen was hot and I wanted to laugh long and loud. After we got outside he took out his handkerchief to wipe his steaming forehead, as he said, "My, my, wasn't that an amazing and entrancing creature. I'll bet she don't play marbles for nothing".

There have been several times in the performance of my duty when life hung by a hair. The most dangerous that I can recall was the curtain-raiser to the famous Dryden Murder case and it was the last act of police work I did as liquor Inspector.

One morning in early May 1930, Chief-of-Police Caldwell called me into his office, looking worried he said, "Cliff, I have a warrant here for a MacDonald, an Irishman believe it or not, who is locked up in Halifax. He is wanted here on a burglary charge and Detective Fox has him on a drunk charge. I can't spare any of the officers to go down for him but I thought you might consider it".

"Well, Chief, I am a sick man and I have been in Halifax twice this week, but I'll go, carry on as long as I can".

"Good, be sure to keep handcuffs on him for he has a dangerous reputation around Sunny Brae."

I took the warrant and went to Halifax on the afternoon train. When I got there I contacted Detective Fox and made arrangements to get him out in time to catch the morning train for New Glasgow. He also warned me to keep the handcuffs on the prisoner.

Through the bars he presented a formidable sight. A hulking bear of a man with a chest like a barrel and heavy thighs and arms. The handcuffs would just snap on his wrist and that was all. We went in a taxi to the depot, then I hustled him into the train. He pleaded with me to take off the cuffs but I kidded him along until we got well along on the road back.

As he told me his story I listened to the richest brogue that had ever come to my ears. He was an Irish immigrant from Galway and had left Queenstown bound for New York to marry his girl, Annie Rooney. The boat had called at Halifax and he had strayed ashore, had missed the boat and had somehow landed drunk in Sunny Brae, Pictou County.

"Sure an'begorre 'tis the devils's mess that I've got into. It's not bracelets I'd be wearin' if I'd stayed on the boat. 'Tis the husband o' swate little Annie Rooney I'd be fer the' banns were published in New York. I stole none o' that shedevil's watches in Sunny Brae. 'Tis my poor ol mither's heart that'l be breakin in old Ireland. Would ye take these cuffs o' my hands. I swear by the blessed soul o' St. Patrick that it's peaceful as a lamb I'll be."

"Would you like to get in touch with Annie Rooney or have you told her where you are?"

"Tis ashamed that I am I have not. Oho, ohone. 'Tis a mess I've got in. And it's not in jail I want to spend my life. But sure an'begorre 'tis only Annie on this side o' the water that can do anything for me, if she still loves me, an' I wouldn't blame her if she didn't. How would the likes o' ye get in touch with her?"

"I wouldn't do it. But when we get to New Glasgow I'll take you to the telegraph office and you can wire her collect, tell her where you are and what you want her to do."

"Glory be to the Saints. And would we be takin' of these cuffs?"

"I'll take a chance. But no funny work or you'll never see or hear from Annie Rooney."

So the handcuffs were unlocked and one of the most picturesque criminals of a generation was taken to the telegraph office in New Glasgow, [and] to jail, where within a short time he was arrested for the murder of Dryden, a hermit, who lived beyond the railroad at Glengarry.

CHAPTER XIV

The Beginning of the End

The agitation for Government Control of the liquor traffic had been growing in intensity throughout 1929. Foreseeing what might happen, I bought a Dodge car, the Dodges having at that time a great reputation for being tough. Politicians promised me a job on the new police force that would be formed but I didn't have the stomach to serve under any officer. I had plotted my own course and had planned my own strategy for too long to be shoved around by any officer. I wanted to be clear of it all and get into some other business. The struggle between Fred Milligan and the rest of the Council had become bitter and it was nerveracking to get the broadsides from both sides. Pressure was put on to raid and railroad bootlegger friends of both sides to the quarrel. In September I managed to get three weeks holidays and with the wife and three friends we went to New York and had a wonderful trip.

The plebiscite on Government Control was held shortly after we got back. The method of carrying it out looked mysterious as all the manipulators of both political parties joined hands to put it down. There was more to this than appeared on the surface so I took a walk down to Dannie's. With his worldly wisdom he would have the correct sights trained on the situation.

"Well, Dannie, it looks as though it was curtains for all the boys and girls in the Trade".

"Right you are, Cliff, and what a setup we are getting. Of course you will be looked after being a good party man, but a lot of us will be left like driftwood on the shore. No use of trying to continue further. The combination against us is too strong." A trace of bitterness crept into his voice, generally so even and placid. It looked worth while getting to the bottom of it.

"How come, Dan? I am baffled by the moves that's going on."

"You saw what happened election day? Deep down the dope is this. The big money men, the men behind the men who run the government, have been looking with envious eyes at the millions being passed around in the illegal liquor traffic. So some bright boys were put to work on propaganda for Government Control, while they, the men behind the scenes schemed out a system that would bring in a steady stream of gold to the bond and stockholders of distilleries and breweries. They will have a bluecoated police force, a naval service yes, and perhaps an airforce to see that no one invades their sanctuary. And all the while the public will go merrily on their way drinking themselves into prosperity."

"I hear that you and Dr. Grant were on the same sides on election day?"

"Certainly. He to protect his job and I to look after mine. I know that when Control comes in I will sell no more rum."

"Strange bedfellows, eh, Dan?"

"No stranger than what we've seen on the other side in this past election. The system of organized hypocracy under which we live makes it imperative for the hangers-on who make a fat living out of the setup to play ball with the powers that be. To be good 'yes' men and to stay in line. So, when we have greed for the dominating motive in our society and organized hypocracy to guard its ramifications, we have created a Frankenstein that may destroy us all. Before the crafty minds behind our system would let go their hold on power they would destroy their enemies, themselves and the world."

"Sometimes I figure it out as we are due for a crackup. What do you think, Dan?"

"The world is dizzy from mushroom prosperity, we seem to be due for a depression."

The crackup was not long delayed. Black Thursday, that terrible October day in 1929 swept away millions of dollars from rich and poor, started the Great Depression of the Hungry Thirties and gave Hitler the green light: it was a day I'll never forget. In New Glasgow's bucket shops the wise guys and the suckers lost their shirts. Standing across the street from the brokers offices that afternoon was to witness some stooped and haggard figures coming out, stonybroke. How could this have happened to us, they would repeat.

I was glad I had followed Dannie's advice and had put the few dollars I had made into real estate. For all over North America people were stunned as stocks moved lower and lower with suicides becoming quite common.

About this time there was an earthquake along the Atlantic seabord that caused a great tidal wave along the Newfoundland and Cape Breton shore. I was sitting in my car outside the police station when the earth could be felt rocking. Soon the firebell rang for different fires from disconnected stove pipes and cracked chimneys. This act of Nature caused the superstitious to be filled with fear and foreboding. It all helped to make that Christmas the most gloomy of years. How different from the bright happy days of 1926!

With the advent of 1930 the quarrel in the council broke into the open. George Grant came out for mayor and was organized against Fred. The row became bitter and to make it worse the Rev. Mr. Service, the Kirk minister began to preach sermons about the corruption of the liquor interests in the town.

Then as town elections rolled around in February, Chadwick, a prominent Liberal and quite a public speaker, was elected.

The orders from the Town Council were to "clean up the town". Particularly Paddy Nolan's because he was a friend of Fred Milligan. They tried to use me as a club to get Fred. His enemies tried to drive him from the council. But he had been a good friend of mine in the days when things were black [and] dreary for me and I could not stab him in the back.

It so happened however, that in a big raid we conducted on Delores' joint that we had the evidence to put a case against her for conducting a bawdy house. Delores was buying a house from Fred on time instalments that she kept protracted because she was foxy enough to realize that there would be an element of protection in such a method. Fred's enemies spread the word that he was the owner of a disorderly house and his wrath came down on me for showing the thing up.

Towards spring we pulled another big raid on the dive and got a man with a bottle of rum he had just bought from Delores and he swore out an affadavit to that effect. He lived on a farm back of Thorburn and said he had to get home to feed his cattle but would come back to town on the day of trial. He didn't show up so I got a benchwarrant for him. This was all big news in the press. What with Rev. Mr. Service thundering in the pulpit, Chadwick orating in the council, the police committee chasing me up for more prosecutions, Fred Milligan bawling me out for turning against him, I was becoming distracted. To add to this while conducting a search for the missing wittness in the slushy woods near Sutherland's river, I caught severe cold and the old pleurisy pains came back.

The situation was becoming impossible and while lying awake at night I saw a procession marching around the bed. Rev. Mr. Service, Chadwick, George Grant the Mayor, Fred Milligan, Dannie MacLennan, Delores, Paddy Nolan, The Queen, Alf Logan, Tom MacKay, Norman MacDonald, they were all there. Then and there I remembered the old strategy, "audacity, audacity and more audacity". If I was to be saved I must be my own savior. The job must be thrown in their teeth. But that would take patience, judgement and proper timing.

Towards the last of April the weather was nice and sunny so I got out on the job again. The hounds were soon yapping at me again but I had a good advisor from an unexpected quarter. While in Magistrate's Sinclair's office getting some papers signed, he looked up with the trace of a smile, and said, "I see they have you in the winepress, Cliff."

"They sure have, sir. If I had my health back I would fight them."

"Don't heed them. I've seen this business operate a long time and anyhow it will soon be over. Let them rave on. What can they do to you?"

Grimly shaking my head I thanked him. It so happened on that same day I met my old friend A.J. Bannerman.

It was cheering to meet him for he had a different slant on things than the ordinary business man. It was common knowledge that lumbermen had lost fortunes with the slump and conditions looked far from rosy with them.

But he still had a smile and a twinkle in his eye as he replied to my greeting. "I feel happy, Cliff. I've lost my earthly accumulations. I've had power, position and money. They are all gone. But I have my health and I can still use an axe and I have a knowledge of the woods. A man can be very happy there. And how are you getting along? I see they are after you."

"The going is tough. You have something that I have lost, health. But during the last four years I have had a lot of fun, I have learned to laugh and I have climbed out of the financial quicksand in which I was stranded. Years ago you gave me some good advice, what would you now do in my case?"

"For what shall it profit a man if he gain the whole world and lose his own soul? The fact is that in the eyes of most people you are not as good as the bootleggers, consequently you can't expect much from the Government. They want to start the new system with a clean sheet. If you are not able to take them by the throat and shake the life out of them, don't expect anything from them. Health is the most important thing, for the rest you'll have to use your own judgement."

"Thanks, A.J. I'll think it over."

To look back on those nerve-wracked days is to wonder how a physical weakling such as I have been could have survived. It may be put down to the inscrutable will of God, Scotch stubborness, and the strategic watchwords of a French revolutionist and a New Glasgow bootlegger.

So I penned my resignation in the following words, — "I, the undersigned hereby tender my resignation as N.S.T.A. Inspector for the Town of New Glasgow because I refuse to be the goat for those in authority".

I signed my name to it and went away on a fishing trip for a week and caught more fish than it has ever been my luck to catch.

The curtains of history were about to swallow up the era of prohibition and an actor in the melodrama was being shuffled off the stage. The castigations I received from the councillors were severe but little did I care. I was free, free, free. I took up the hammer and saw, worked on my own account and got back a measure of health, something that I needed and prized throughout the Hungry Thirties. The Dryden Murder case broke with all its absurd detective blunders and as a public official I was soon forgotten. Such is life.

DIARY OF CLIFFORD ROSE

Dec. 30, 1925. Have bought this book for the purpose of jotting down occasional impressions of the passing world as we journey to the grave. Almost twenty years since I gave up this interesting habit. Life in the meantime has passed its zenith leaving shattered illusions shattered opinions and shattered idols. But, withal, having a somewhat varied experience and a small understanding of human nature, can agree with the preachers. All is vanity and vexation of spirit. And with Amor Khayan. A bowl of wine, etc., make the people laugh at the right time and make them drop a sympathetic tear and if their opinion of you is to be valued at all you'll stand a trifle above zero in their estimation . . . .

Am working on the Sharon [?] Church. Have been there since August. A good steady job, a good crowd as crowds go and nice work . . . .

Dec. 31, 1925 . . . . Am totalling up amount earned last year. I find that I made $916.00 made up as follows:

Jan.	70.00	May	80.00	Sept.	94.50
Feb.	15.00	June	75.00	Oct.	120.00
March	85.00	Aug.	80.00	Dec.	105.00

Have put 10 tons of coal in cellar during past year.

Jan 3 . . . . Buried Sam Turner, the self-styled "famous painter and decorator". Had a large funeral on New Years day. Had a celebration New Years night at Jim McDougall's. Old Mr. McDougall there. What a tribe of children, grandchildren and great-grandchildren. Remarkable. Hospitality their motto.

Jan. 10 . . . . Father took a weak turn in Murdock's blacksmith's shop. Heartbreaking sight when I arrived. Hard and mean all his life, hard and mean in the end. "Chill penury repressed their noble joye and froze the genial current of their soul".

Penury, poverty, provincial hard luck, lack of imaginative and courageous endeavour, clear reasoning and lying politicians, these are some of the reasons why this country is in the rut.

Jan. 11. 1 ton coal.

Jan. 12 . . . . Coal commission hands down report. If both parties to contract would accept same prosperity would be ours. Wild time in House of Commons at Ottawa. Very interesting. J.J. Fraser, Druggist runs for mayor. Solicits my support as pillar for this ward.

Jan. 17 . . . . Government returned in House of Commons by 3 majority. First degree in lodge tomorrow night . . . .

Jan. earned $72.00.

Feb. 15 . . . . Jim Grant has gone teach [sic] to the United States last

Monday. Aunt Myrtle went away Thursday morning.

Feb. 27. Nothing much to record last two weeks. Church finished Mon. Feb. 15. Opened Tuesday, Feb. 21 . . . . Have been working at oddfellows clubroom since. Paid J.J. Grant $5.00 on note Feb. 23. Paid insurance today. Having some difficulty getting sum of $47.25 due me on the Church.

Earned $63.00 during February.

March 7. Am 37 years old today. How little do we realize the passing of the years. Celebrated it by inviting McFadgns and we sure had a spread fit for a King. Also had some grand music from some records procured at J.S. Fraser's sale. Have built in a refrigerator and made some other odds and ends. Received money due me from Church after raising a row with Dan A. March 6 1 ton coal.

March 14 . . . . Had a very pleasant surprise at the house last Wednesday. 43 people here celebrating 10th wedding anniversary. Chair presented to us. Very nice and comfortable. Didn't earn a dollar this week.

March 17. St. Patricks and a lonely day . . . . Tore down old henhouse. Preacher visited here today. I was at a cornboil at McFagdns' last night.

March 31 . . . . Have been working on D.R. McKay's garage in Antigonish. Boarding house full of Gaelic . . . . Am out of work at present . . . . Coal — $7.20 March 31. Earned $55.00 this month.

April 12. Have had the rotten job of Temperance Act inspector for one week. The inside of New Glasgow is rotten to the core. Rum dives are thick as bees. Have had a lot of fun raiding them . . . .

April 27 . . . . Got evidence on Mrs. Neuman Betts today. Earned $72.00 in April.

May 7 . . . . Fencing up home. Amusing but vulgar trial of John Dumas. Made first batch Hires root beer . . . .

May 8 . . . . Raided five dives today. Had some fun with the niggers on the banjos at Clarence Sheppard's.

May 28. Time flies very fast on this job. Am beginning to like it better. Main thing is not to be sneaky and not to be scared. Have an interesting opium case on hand at present time . . . .

June 12 . . . . I have got foolish myself and have bought a new car. Don't know if I can ever pay for it or not. So far have been very successful in the Liquor game. Steel works threatens to close down for good . . . . Chief Osborne of the Police Force resigns.

July 6. Have had some interesting experiences since last report. Fancy raid on Mrs. Margaret McKenzie South Street. She smashes the toilet in order to get clear of the evidences of rum. Also raid on Laura Robertson. Fined. Doug Gbrame [Graham] there.

Have had a trip to Canso with Tom McKay. Beautiful scenery. Quite a time at Frenchman's picnic. Earned $130.00 last month. Coal $7.20.

July 18. Have had some very interesting trips and experiences lately. Find keg of rum with the Indians at Pine Tree. Circus in town July 16. Very orderly. James Chisholm convicted.

Aug. 29. Find it has been over a month since I have jotted down anything worth while. Life has been very exciting at certain points. In July H.R. Grant takes a notion to raid. We have some excitement at Dan McLellans. Some one drops case of rum from attic window at H.R. Grant's feet. We raid Roger and Cliff McDougalls.

Have had a holiday in Charlottetown. Mrs. Keinan, Nina and Gwyn are nice people. Election excitement slow. Election on 14th of Sept. Was down to Antigonish other night. Crafty John C. Douglas has a chance to win.

Amy Mason, "Queen of the Bootleggers" has flown the coop. Caught at Ballantyne's Cove with car load of Rum.

August earned $130.00.

Sept. 21. Some time has elapsed since we last reported. Have had eight days in Guysboro Co. previous to election. The way Cape Bretoners run elections isnt slow. John C. Douglas elected. He is some crafty politician. Meighen govt defeated. Probably best thing for the country . . . . Have had some delightful drives with the car this summer. Down to Cape George, Ballantynes Cove, Sunny Brac. Wonderful scenery. Nothing doing in rum circles these times except some raids in Pictou. Pictou exhibition poorly attended . . . .

September earned $135.00. Coal $14.40. Wood $4.50.

Oct. 17 . . . . Had long drives last two days serving supreme court papers. Was down to Lower Barney's River today. Got Hallet Casey Oct. 4. Had some experience in Casey's. Smashed open door. Found room full of travellers.

Earned $140.00 in Oct. Coal $7.20.

Nov. 11. Armistice day . . . . Drove with Walter Weir down to Abercrombie. Got ditched. Was over to Truro. Thanksgiving Day. Was down to Pictou today. Bad fire last night at Lem Mills. Two houses burned. Cap of Acadia Coal Co. watchman found on road. Supposed to be James [?].

. . . . Got Duncan Stewart and Ken Mason last month.

Have just been reading over interesting records of this last year. Sometimes I wonder why I havent been shot. And as I read this one I realize that I have changed somewhat myself. This is a job for a fox. Crookedest game on earth. Things I would scorn a year ago, I would do quite easily now. But it is wonderfully exciting and dramatic at times.

Nov. 20 . . . . Was serving summons in Case Rex vs. Deagle. . . . .
Have been steadily at work on case of Rex vs. Deagle. On Monday night
Nov. 15 Jack Murray was robbed at Middle River. He requested me to act
with him in Case. Hunting criminals is a very tired [sic] and weary job
although exciting. They were run down in Westville. Trial Monday Nov.
22. Convicted James Gale today.

Alfred Wilson's wife died this week. Catholic funeral. Mussolini, by
the press, proves himself biggest man in our generation. Some hard nut.

Nov. 28. After two days trial case adjourned for judgement Sat. Nov.
27. Criminals sent up for supreme Court. Feel somewhat elated because
Tom McKay and Robt. Douglas were working against me. Spreading all
kinds of rumours . . . .

Fierce fire last night in McLellan's Furniture Store. Alarm rang at
12. Continued for six hours. Drenched with water and smoke. A bad fire.
Had some exciting moments.

Earned during November $175.00. Coal $7.20.

Dec. 19 . . . . Dec. 5th was out all afternoon delivering summons of
Deagle Daly case . . . . John C. Douglas died Friday night. A Clever
Politician but unscrupulous as Hell. Rev. D.K. Grant stages some imita-
tion high-class detective work in securing liquor for convictions. Mrs.
Laura Robertson has him arrested for assault. His case come up Tuesday.
Report of Duncan Commission handed down in Parliament. Wonder
whether it will make history or not.

. . . . Put the car in the garage for the winter last Sunday. Had the best
summer of my life. Interesting, colourful and romantic for an old bird.
Nothing like Amor Khayan for sound Philosophy if one is heady enough
to carry it.

Dec. 19. Had very interesting week. Cases of Halifax detectives in
booze trials come up. They are subjected to heavy cross examinations by
R. Douglas Gbrame [Graham]. So severe is public opinion and severity of
defence council that they dramatically withdraw cases.

Public are overwhelmingly on our side. I win my two cases. Mrs.
Neuman Betts, one victim gives evidence on stand that Mr. Rose likes to
put his arms around a fat woman.

Fred Sherry arrested for allowing drunkenness on his premises. Also
his fancy lady, Mrs. C-----. Remember when she was a pretty fair-haired
kid. Daughter of Pete J--------. Very sad the sight she made when arrested.

John C. Douglas buried with great honour. His going shows that the
loyalty of the Highland Scotch for a departed chief still survives. Dastard-
ly attack on the dead by Jas. A. Fraser in Eastern Chronicle brings public
disapproval.

Monday, Dec. 28. Almost a year since I started this diary. Am glad that I have continued to do so. Have had a splendid Xmas. Got a beautiful watch from Stan Fraser as well as many other nice presents. . . .

Well this has probably been the most successful year in my life. "I've had my whack of feast and fun" and I've had a wonderful experience in life. Have learned that law and justice are two different things. And when I see the things that are pulled in a small town, what must it be in a big city. And this morning stipendiary A.M. Fraser dismissed a case against Fred Sherry because the law was Ultra Vires and that the legislature had no power to pass such a law.

Dec. earned $145.00. One ton coal $7.20.

Jan. 1, 1927. New Years Day. Was to the show "Way Down East" with the kids . . . . After reading over my opinions and jottings of last year I realize I had made a mistake when I said that life has passed its zenith last year. Have had the best year I've ever had in my life. Both financially, physically and from the point of experience and seeing the country . . . . Got Jim Fellow yesterday. This is my reckoning for last year's financial returns. Got 12 tons coal this last year.

Jan.	$ 72.00	July	$130.00
Feb.	63.00	Aug.	130.00
Mar.	55.00	Sept.	135.00
April	72.00	Oct.	140.00
May	125.00	Nov.	175.00
June	115.00	Dec.	145.00
		Total	$1357.00

Jan. 9 . . . . Had Jim Fellow convicted yesterday. His rum ordered analyzed by magistrate. Am inspecting the remodelling of court House.

Jan. 16 . . . . Have had a trip to Halifax to get analysis of rum obtained in dwelling of James Fellow. Attorney General Hall very pleasant man to meet.

Have had an interesting time inspecting remodelling of old Court House. I wonder if some future lover of cleanliness will ever be able to picture the filthy state in which our Town dignatories have been satisfied to conduct courts of law. Will [sic] come or go I am the one who advocated a change — and its for the best. Times are slack in general but business in Canada appears to be brightening up . . . .

Jan. 25 . . . . Attending County Court today.

Got George Cavanagh Sat. night. Fred Milligan more than pleased. Earned $125.00 this month. 1 ton coal.

Feb. 1 . . . . Mother taken to hospital last Friday with pneumonia. Very sick and miserable. Worn out and weary with working and worrying on a damd old Nova Scotia farm. Have I put many wrinkles on her furrowed forehead? I can conscienciously say no. And right out loud. Its just the misery of living, of worrying about saving a dollar and of looking out for my father a hard old miser. The fear of the grim old scotch Prysbyterian's God. Some Monster. Have I done anything to ease out that furrowed face. Not what I should have done. I'll not attempt to set down any Alibis. Great Osiris is that feather light or heavy? Old Alex Wilson is also in the hospital. A tough old grizzly bear. Mean as hell. Ye Gods what a mean breed that old creed made of people. No wonder Nova Scotia is like a beggar sitting on a bag of gold . . . .

Feb. 6. Since writing the last my mother died. My best friend in life has departed. Its hard to put ones impressions on paper. First I never thought the going of my parents would happen in this way. I always thought that my father would go first and that she could enjoy a little while of comfort. For by all the Gods it was coming to her. Alas the mystery of fate or is it just blind unreasoning chance. Cold and Hard as the granite. Remorseless as a Juggernaut. Poor foolish mortals that we be. Old Ecclesiastes and Amor Khayan are nearer right than any . . . .

Feb. 13. Well one week has past since mother died. I stopped writing the last entry to go and help carry her body into the house . . . . I took the preacher Mr. Lowrie from Antare out to comfort my father. Not that I care for religion but others do.

Have had several drives out into the country this last week on raids. One nigger carved another with razor on street last night.

Feb. 27 . . . . Had some excitement on a raid on McNeil's dive in Westville. Like a moving picture for a few minutes. When we came out Matt Richardson, town councillor had three cans of rum which had been thrown out of the window. He was convicted last Wednesday.

One ton coal earned $120.00.

March 7. Birthday today. 38 years of age . . . .

Old Alex Wilson about ready to come out of hospital. Am trying to negotiate his removal. He wishes to come and live with us. But is stingy as hell about paying for it. Well I am not fussy about his coming. If he comes it will be worth while for he is a contrary-minded man.

March 13 . . . . Alex Wilson came to terms and signed agreement for two years. Signed same on March 9. It is a great relief to have the where-withal to wipe off my bills.

Had some excitement last night between 12 and one raided Cecil Roop on Marsh Street. Found him feeding Whiskey to a McKenzie from Pictou. Mrs. Ben S----- setting on McKenzie's knee. Furious assault for a few minutes. Took Roop down to jail.

March 20 . . . . Cecil Roop convicted yesterday. John D. Grant new magistrate went up in the air when Roop's friends tried to use political influence.

April 3 .... Was out at Mother's grave today .... It's a cruel world. The misery and agony of human blindness and lack of knowledge and the unalterable fact that life spawns in the gutters and that crime and violence continue to grow while intelligence and reason are slow to perpetuate their kind.

As I grow older I firmly believe that [sic] the old-fashioned virtues of loyalty to one's friends, telling the truth and common courtesy to all. The triangle of sound civilization.

Stan Fraser appealed the Roop case. No decision from Judge as yet. Big scare on among the bootleggers tonight.

Had a thorough search of Ken Mason's yesterday. Lots of evidences but no rum.

Earned in March $130.00. 2 tons of coal.

April 10 .... Had some excitement last night. Got quart of rum in cellar of Mrs. Neuman Betts. Sneaked around rooms of great war vets. Got in quick but no rum. Ha — a very good hiding place. Have been on this job for a year now. And have learned a lot. Have got a trifle hard, but not crusted over. Gave a broken Englishman, dead broke, 1/2 a dollar ....

Yes the year just gone by has been the most successful in my life from a worldly point of view. From thrift, so called "graft" and Old Alex's money. I have a car almost payed for. Old debts squared off and money in the bank.

Also infinitely wiser in craftiness. The ways and wiles of the law are fast finding out.

April 16. Have seen a wonderful picture "Over the Hill", at Roseland. How true to life it is. They say that the righteous are never forsaken. Well the old Mathews couple over eighty have been taken to the poor house and I have known them to be thoroughly good and religious and they have come to that.

It was wonderful how that picture brings back ones boyhood and spurs ones conscience.

April earned $155.00. Coal one ton ....

May 2. Find some time has flown since I recorded anything of note. Have been painting house between spurts. Have had an unexpected raise in pay. Am now getting $120.00 per month. Took in $1000.00 in fines this month. This is a record. A tidy salary with the extras. Took down James W. Fraser of Marshdale last Wed. A horrible case of Cancer in the nose and gone into his brain .... Took a prisoner up from Pictou this afternoon.

May 9. Was down to Pictou by ten mile house. First time this year. Roads in great condition. Had some excitement with the Indians at Pictou landing. Drunk and fighting.

Was up to see my Aunt Mary at Plymouth yesterday afternoon. She has been a hell of a hard-worked woman. Those old breed of men were women slave drivers. As far as husbands go the world is improving.

. . . . Spend 2½ hours raiding Casey last night. Couldnt get any rum but he decided to pay up today.

May 24 . . . . Jim McKay's house on West side burned today. Had three convictions last night. With Tom McKay and Chief McLanders of Pictou we "get" Dave Morrison of Pictou last night . . . .

June 5. Have been easing up on the rum-element last while. Had a good trip to Mulgrave ten days ago . . . . Rotary ministrel show over.

June 19 . . . . Have started the rabbit business with Tom McKay. Was down to Bridgemouth last weekend and bought 6. I guess the guy we bought them from "lifted us". But he done it to us with our eyes open. So the fault is ours. We are keeping them at Alex Dunbars farm.

House burglaries are the thorn in the side of the police this summer. Have been losing a lot of sleep over them. Caldwell the Chief slipped away and Langille has the burden. Is working his head off. But his methods depend on level-headed luck. The process of elimination to my mind is better. . . .

July 2. Have been in the house with a touch of muscular rheumatis [sic] the last few days. Confederation celebrations on. Kind of flat, however. Wm. Chisholm, florist out Little Harbour Rd and Don Sinclair had their flags at half mast yesterday. Its peculiar how an idea will survive. But the trouble could have been better fixed by rebellion sixty years ago. But the Highlands will stick to forlorn Hopes.

. . . . Had the family down at a Margaree harbour. Here's hoping they wont strike it [oil]. For it is a beautiful sight the trout leaping in the Margaree at Sunset. If oil is struck all the beauty will vanish as at Inverness the meanest looking town in Nova Scotia.

Just earned $210.00. Aug. $135.00.

Sept 11. Find that almost six weeks have gone by since I have jotted anything down. Well there hasnt been much to jot down except a record of recovery, relapse, pain, agony, and a fight for another recovery. Its a long hard road for another steady streak of health.

Not much of interest in the rum game except Tom McKay getting into a snarl over the report that his car was the one that got away at Sutherlands river when Meaghr and Anderson were caught with a load of rum. The Eastern Chronicle has made capital of it and will get into a libel suit. . . .

Oct. 5. Have at last come back on duty. Its great to have friends. Have been paid full salary since I have been sick. Was down to the Fergusson lakes at Chance Harbour. A lovely spot. Wonderful for a summer cottage.

Well tis over three months since I have been out at night and they have flown speedily. Old Alex Wilson left us some three weeks ago. Told us he didn't get enough to eat . . . .

Oct. 9. Had a beautiful drive today through West River valley and back past the famous Church at Gairloch. It is a noble institution — newly painted. The Ku-Klux-Klan met there last Thursday night for church service. What Scottish memories and stories could be told around that famous old Church . . . .

Oct. 15 . . . . Had the satisfaction of catching Cameron Johnston at his beer sitting yesterday. Have issued warrant. Hope that he will leave the country.

Oct. 30 . . . . Have got an occasional attack of pleurisy pains. Have been going to a chropactor [sic] for treatments did some good. Got phone call the other night to raid Jack Campbell's as Mabel R---- (Peter S-------'s the Master's wife) was drunk there. Fought shy of it as we had gone to school together. Paddy Nolan the hockey player, on account of hard times etc. has opened a rum joint. Poor Paddy. D.K. Grant raided him last week but got nothing.

Have been reading over my past records and how small how comparatively little space our lives can be compressed into. I have forgotten to record that I have had a nice granite stone erected at my mother's grave. She had a few blood-soaked dollars saved up and when in life she always had a dread of indecent burial caused by the meanness of my father . . . . Physically I'm not the man I used to be but I find that my brain works clear as a bell. Have had a very successful month in my prosecution but find that the situation has slipped somewhat during my sickness. Thank goodness I can think clear.

Nov. 14 . . . . took George Smith, coloured to Pictou for assaulting a white girl. He got a letter in the jail warning him that his end was near. Tom McKay and I have a row over his getting a fine from Paddy Nolan, popular Hockey player and good Tory worker, who had to sell rum because the weak kneed local representatives could not get him a job. Feeling runs high with Fred Milligan at bat. Good friend, Fred but a bitter enemy. Got a new closed car last week. More rum money so they say anyhow. Wife went away on trip to St. John last week. Veria [?] says it would not do for me to put down all that happens in this book.

Dec. 2 . . . . Have had some experience in the game of wits the last few weeks which has taught me a few lessons. Some that I knew before but never appreciated . . . . And where are wits better employed than in the illegitimate game of handling rum.

Dec. 11 . . . . Buddie's dog, Rover, was killed with a car last night. His heart is nearly broke. Also Myrtle's. It is Buddie's first real taste of the tragedy of life. Of which I can write nothing new. The dog grew up with them the last two years and after all the feelings of a dog towards their friends are genuine which is more than can be said of human beings as a whole.

An instance of this comes to mind in Tom McKay. District Deputy Liquor Inspector. Someone has written that man is half-God and half-beast. A year ago he was a good friend and a good fellow, today he is greed personified. Slashing friends right and left. What a hell of a thing is greed or human acquitiveness [sic]. A monster a hellish monster. I am glad that I have had pleurisy because in enforced convalescence I had time to clear my brain.

Jan. 6 . . . . Quite a war has broken out in the conservative party over Tom McKay's crookedness. He thought that he owned everything for his benefit. That he had a stream of gold flowing into his pocket. That we all were servants for his acquisitiveness. This war has come [to] bloodshed between Walter Weir and Paddy Nolan. Paddy is an old hockey player and he put it over Walter.

Jan. 22 . . . . A whole week has gone by without a crime of any kind recorded in the courthouse. Nothing doing in temperance circles either. Tom McKay's gang had it put over them in political battle. Our gang for the meantime victorious. How they are crawling towards us with niceness. It is amusing. Beau Geste and Ben-Hur two great moving pictures have just concluded a run here . . . .

Performed a little Beau Geste myself toward Cameron Johnston whom I had sent to jail for selling beer. He wanted a copy of my new booklet "Before the Hector" while we were conveying him to Pictou. We also were having a sing-song on our trip down there. On the inside of the flyleaf, I penned a note to him in commemoration of our pilgrimmage to Pictou and my uncertain rendering of "The Lord is my shepherd".

Feb. 5 . . . . Had a sad case yesterday. Had to take two boys to St. Patrick's Home Halifax. Lived with the Grandfather of 80. Grandmother had died last October. Mother had died last October. Had to carry one of them from under bed. Then carry him to the train. A boy of 15. His Home was destitute and absolutely barren. But he cried for it. "Home Sweet Home" . . . .

Feb. 12. Big snowstorm the last three days. The town is keeping the streets open with the tractor. We again have control of the council. Fred Milligan plays a hard game. He asks for no quarter and he gives none. Had a great time at the fireman's dance. Had two sets of lancers with Belle Roy a slick dancer and a nice girl. We had our uniforms on and along with evening dresses of the ladies, very snappy.

Had a somewhat hectic afternoon. I locked up Mike Hanoven for being drunk. Apparently he got it from the building on George Street. We raided it and found four quarts of rum and two quarts of whiskey.

March 6 . . . . Had a hectic attack from the Eastern Chronicle last week. Did not know that I was worth so much in their pages. Guess I will decide tomorrow about going to a prominent lawyer in Halifax about putting the curb on him. Also big raids last week by the Federal Officers. They got liquor in four places. Cliff McDougall the big calf had his rum in his taxi office. I told him not to on several occasions. He pled guilty when I told him not to. So I cracked him under the chin for a fine. Also had a moral effect on the other three to make them fight. Its a hell of a game this rum game . . . .

March 6 [sic]. Tomorrow is my birthday. Thirty nine years of age. Only lately have I noticed a few grey hairs while my fellow strugglers in the case are bald and thick in the girth. But I have deteriorated in bodily physique because of weakness of the lungs, constipation etc. But my will power and ability to think clearly is better than ever. And an abiding faith in being loyal to friends is growing stronger as the years roll by. Though I must say that in a squeeze some of our friends love to have the laugh on us.

One thing is puzzling to me and I sometimes laugh at my foolishness. But it is amazing how I can get solid with women and girls with whom if I was the man I was 12 years ago, I never get a look in. Sometimes I wonder how far they are "kidding" me. But it has a kick to it anyhow. And I never cross the line. And I always remember the ones who will be with me when girls will pass me up if I live long enough.

But as I see life more and more of a game, why the dears are a mighty interesting part.

April 26. Some seven weeks have elapsed since I have written the last note. When I saw a steady period of protracted illness ahead of me I took steps out of this evil climate. First thought of going to the British West Indies. But on the advice of Walter McNeil I went to North Carolina by way New York and it certainly has been the holiday of my life. New York is a mighty city and it sort of hits one between the eyes. North Carolina is a nice country. People seem to be just folks. Kindly people but touchy. They have the old southern hospitality that to be appreciated must be known. Was also in Akron and saw James Grant.

Met an intelligent woman in North Carolina. It is so long since this has occurred before that it was a treat to discuss philosophy with her. And she had brains and initiative also.

It is also too soon to give any definite impressions of the trip but one fact stands out and that is that the Americans are an ignorant people as far as world affairs are concerned. Money is their God. To get it is their chief end of life. The south is a bit different. They have time to be courteous.

Had quite an adventure with a drunken broker on the train coming home from Montreal. My money was no good when I fell in with him. I took him away from a bunch of Chicago fishermen who were making sport of him. He gave me some good advice concerning the stock market. I am wondering how it will turn out.

Surprised some of the schemers when I came home by jumping in and raiding Clarence McDermid and getting him good, with three drums of alcohol and six bags of beer.

May 12. Have had another jam with Tom McKay. He spitefully raided Paddy Nolans cache and we trimmed him in court. He crawled like a big galoot. Have done some little speculation on the stock market. Some fortunate . . . . Budd, A.P. Ross [?], McCann and I were down fishing at Kelties Lake last Wednesday. It was worth more than money to hear Buddies shouts as he hauled in his first fish . . . .

Old Uncle Bill has been kicked about badly. Hope that I can do something to keep him out of the poor house. Mother wouldn't like it.

May 27 . . . . Was out on a fishing trip with Langille and Fred Milligan last week. At the Gunn Bros camp at Long Lake in the Barrens. The Gunns are fine men for rich people. They made the foundation of this fortune in the Klondike. They are real men. And have travelled a great deal. Despite Fred Milligans wealth he has never had a holiday like that before . . . . Town was busy from a musical standpoint last night. Three dances and an industrial fair going on. Raided Joe Hoke. He lives in a dugout in his cellar.

My chief comment on that fishing trip is how different it has been from the beastly ones with Tom McKay.

June 10 . . . . Have been painting the house. Also have taken to playing softball. Feel my strength returning. In fact feel better than I have for a long time. Dr. Wadland was the Chropractor [sic] who advised me what to eat . . . . Got 25 gals of rum down on ballast island last sunday night. Quite an experience. Saw a mob of women besieging McCulloch and Potters [?] sale last Thursday. Scary how women chase after bargains.

July 1st . . . . Have been very busy last few weeks. Crime flourishing. Trying to track down the cottage smashers at Pictou Landing. I havent got luck at crime but have some at rum. The principal elements of success in tracking down criminals is perseverance and luck.

. . . . Central parking grounds opened in shipyard.

July 11 . . . . Was up to the picnic at Gairloch this afternoon. Real old Scotch time. Does ones heart good. Immense crowd there. Have bought Fred Milligan's cottage at Pictou Landing. Three young devils of kids in it.

July 23 . . . . Have often been thinking of writing a book on rum trade but idea has always been hazy. It is now beginning to take form. Dont know if I shall ever be able to bring it down to earth or not. Got Belle Roy to type and correct some stories I wrote years ago and sent them in to McLean's magazine in a story contest. Just for luck.

Aug. 12 . . . . Have off and on been constructing plan of story "Great God Rum". A difficult problem, requiring craftmanship. Hope to make it realistic. If I have the leisure and feel O.K. bodily, I believe I can make some kind of a job.

Aug. 17 . . . . Big excitement in town over the jailing of Walter McNeil. They gave him a dirty rap unjustly.

Sept. 29. Weather continues very fine. We have had a wonderful summer. I was feeling fine and getting real kittenish playing softball etc but this damd job has its nerve wrecking occasions. And I am not as good as I was. Saw the diggers in the new Metropolitan store on back street digging up the logs that once were the foundations of a bridge over the creek running up into market square. Sound as a bell.

Have been working on the story off and on since two months. It is beginning to assume shape. Some parts of it are good. It all depends on how I can polish it. Elections in on Monday. Things are very quiet.

Oct. 10. This day have seen the last softball game of season. Weather continues very fine. Was down to Big Island duck fishing yesterday. The woods are gorgeous. In all my life I never remember of a summer in which the conditions of life and nature have been better. In spite of a degree of ill health I have enjoyed this past year. It has been full of good things . . . .

Oct. 29 . . . . My father is nearby his last . . . . Poor old man. He never worried. Penuriousness drove him into a hard frozen rut. Ye Gods what a life my mother dead and gone, put in slaving for him and us all. Strange the contrariness of fate! And how short Oh how short is human life and what is the use of money grabbing and cheating. My father was a peculiar man. He was in a way well-read. Some of my life's delights in reading can be traced back to his fireside tales of "Bonnie" (Napoleon Bonnepart) and the early days of hunting and fishing when game was plenty. And he could tell stories. Often have I gone to bed in the "loft" of the old house trembling with thrills of wonder and fear from his peculiar stories . . . .

For years I was a petulant bad-tempered young man. I hated him for his unprogressiveness and his meaness to my mother who was a restless striver to get along. I turned against him — naturally I suppose. So that young spirit was hidden by the years.

I have missed a lot by it. During the last few years I have often went up to the old home intending to get him started again but my sister has his hardness without his romantic flights of favor.

The spirit of the house killed my good intentions. I have boarded up the Old House. Another tragedy —

Well I have finished writing "The Great God Rum" and it is a good yarn. Have given it to Belle Roy to type. Strange how that smart clever girl is the only one to whom I could cheerfully confide the gut of the matter. But somehow she understands things. A real nice girl. Straight as a string.

The "Graf Zeppelin" flew from Germany to Lakehurst the other day. Quite an event. Twenty passengers and over fifty of a crew.

Oct. 31 Halloween. My father died this morning. Poor old man he led a peaceful uneventful life. Only once outside of Pictou County and eighty years of age.

Nov. 3. Opened father's old chest last night. What old relicks, locks of hair of women dead and gone. Fragments of love-letters etc. and still the stream of being flows forward. It made me depressed and I took a stiff hooker of scotch when I got home — something rare for me to do.

Nov. 25 . . . . Spent the other night spearing the river for rum supposed to be buried in channel. Hunting smugglers sure has a kick. It was a perfect night.

Started a bungalow on Carleton Street. Got three lots for $300.00 The old town is looking up again. Two years work in sight at the carworks so I decided to make a stab at it. . . .

Last week sent away to the Canadians Magazine copy of "The Great God Rum". I wonder what luck I'll have. I never have had luck in anything but Rum and as for other things they have been run-of-mine.

Got in a celler for a bungalow on Carleton St. I hope to leave this damd job soon and can have something to work at.

Dec. 25. Xmas again and a black ground one at it. Old Santa has been very kind however. Got some very nice presents however. A pair of woolen mitts from Mike Hubard, an old town labourer for whom I often gave a bottle of rum to cheer his weary soul. I appreciate that very much. . . .

Had a disagreeable duty to perform yesterday. Had to take Cammy Cummings to Pictou. A harmless oldtimer in town who got behind in his board.

. . . . H.R. Grant was on the war path yesterday.

Jan. 12, 1929. Find that I have not made any entry for the New Year as yet. Well last year was a very prosperous year for me as far as worldly prosperity is concerned. Also have derived mental benefit by writing the story "The Great God Rum". Walter McNeil, wealthy financier and literateur criticized it with his penetrating mind and I have again corrected it and have obtained Miss Bell Roy with her bright intelligent mind to type it. I wonder what its fate shall be. I am satisfied myself that it is a good story.

Had two second offence cases in the courts lately. Both were dismissed And I'm glad of it. Obtained $5600.00 for the town last year. Everybody appears satisfied except for the prohibition cranks.

Had a touching incident come home to me last week when taking Robert Fraser from a lonesome farm on McLennan's mountain to the insane asylum at Dartmouth. When he was about to enter the portals he turned around and said "Goodbye, blessed sun. Goodbye trees, goodbye God and everything".

. . . . Got the chimney of the bungalow finished. Also the roof.

. . . . Norman McKay, a son of squire MacKay of the old stone house died last Tuesday. A fine old man. Quite a few of the old timers have passed out this winter. A black winter is never healthy.

Feb. 10 . . . . Got the bungalow finished on the outside. Billy Bangley found it fine enough to paint it on the outside.

Fireman's annual ball last Friday night. As usual had a whale of a time. Had an annual set of dances with Bell Roy. How that girl can dance! . . . .

March 17 . . . . Well the perennial war between the rival factions in the town has broken out again between Tom McKay and Fred Milligan. Tom McKay is the last word in a master crook as we understand them. But he overplayed his hand — got drunk and raided Paddy Nolan, Milligan's right hand man and leading sportsman. The Eastern Chronicle has a beautiful masterpiece of literature in the shape of a write up.

What stories I could write of the life I've seen if I could only get an opening! Four of our Bootleggers have passed in their checks this winter. The strain is too hard on them.

Received back the story "The Great God Rum" for second time with nice letter. It's hard to understand why people dont appreciate literature. Ha Ha

April 7 . . . . The combat between the McKay-Milligan factions continues to wage, sometimes fierce but just now, there is a lull. If anything we have the edge on them. Its a dirty war consisting of foils, strategies and artifices. Have been reading Napier's History of the Peninsula war and at times have adopted some of Wellington's tactics. Namely "never assume an offensive without securing a safe line of retreat" . . . .

April 22 . . . . Some excitement in town last week. Owing to the agitations by the advocasy of Catholic separate schools the K.K.K. at midnight on April 17 burnt four crosses on several hills around the town. Catholics and niggers very scared.

Times are much better than they have been for some years. New cars are out in force and a vaudeville bill has been run at the Academy for some five weeks.

May 1 . . . . Was up to Glengarry with the car yesterday . . . . What a forsaken neighbourhood. Good houses falling into disusatitude [sic]. Only a few old couples here and there. Jas H. Power was evidently of a lonesome nature learning that I was attempting to scribble very generously asked me to a long conflab on literary matters. Well he has the luck with him and writes fairly well. I havent got the luck in that game . . . .

May 24th. I took a crazy man to Dartmouth. Took Mike Hubard along as assistant. First holiday he had ever had for 35 years. Took him to see the talking picture which have just started in Halifax. Perhaps he didnt enjoy himself! Mike is a genuine faithful employee of the town of New Glasgow and Im glad I gave him a good time. Was out to the lakes in the Barren last week. Fierce weather.

However we got a good catch at Kelties. 85 between us.

June 21 . . . . Am getting the shack at the shore repaired. Have got an old Dodge car now. Lots of room to move in it.

Women are funny. My little friend Bell Roy had a crush on a new comer to town. Wanted me to find out if he was O.K. But everybody thought him a regular guy. Darned if I didnt get a divorce notice to serve on him from his wife in Sydney. I tipped off Belle and she hasnt forgiven me yet even though she shook Morrison . . . .

July 18 . . . . Large number of American cars on the street. Now Norfolk Hotel in course of construction . . . .

Some time ago some of us on the police force put through a coup in a manner that would do credit to Machavelli. Old McCann an ignorant old bugger on the police force always carrying news to Tom McKay and trying to get fresh with women far above him, was a thorn in the flesh. He knew a lot that was dangerous. And how to get clear of him was the problem. But it was done. He sunk and only a few bubbles came up.

Aug. 16 . . . . Halifax raiders (Fenian Raiders) have been searching for booze. The[y] "got" old Mother Robertsons. But through scinivicating I got the fine first. Ive got to be some slipperly gent. Well its do or be done unto.

Little George G---- built a swell house this summer for his wife May Blue. But May always was a peppy girl and couldn't live without "whooping her up" so she held a wild party — rum, women and song — when George walked in the middle of it. Doug Clish was strumming the uke in the centre of the floor and G---- fetched him a sweet kick on the ass and sent him spinning. I saw the end of the fracus when May chased him with a butchers knife.

And I forgot to mention that after I fined Mrs. Robertson I wrote a great letter of flattery for her daughter about to graduate in Boston and it was printed in the news.

Aug. 26 . . . . Have had a peculiar case in court lately. The old Highland fighting spirit is not dead yet. Some two years ago Garnet Brine candy dealer in Antigonish was knocked out by Red McDurwold from Lismore. This summer Brine hired two of the Cobalt MacDonalds to beat up Red. They laid for him but he beat them up. Then Brine got drunk, hired eight hard men and went out to Red's. They awakened him and his brother but Red was there again for on the first charge 3 men went down. The two brothers beat up the eight then swore out a warrant for Brine, for committing a riot. I arrested Brine and he had a beautiful pair of Black Eyes. Case was adjourned because the information was made out wrong for one man cannot be charged with committing a riot.

Great excitement in the press for the Graf Zeppelin has completed the trip around the world.

Sept. 1 . . . . Corner of Trinity Church laid today. Rev. Clarence McKinnon of the oily tongue preached the sermon.

Oct. 2 Find that a month has gone by since the last entry. Well along with the wife and Mr. and Mrs. Ches Ervine [?] had a very good trip to New York. Weather was very fine. Saw all the sights . . . .

The city monument to returned men unveiled last week. Very nice.

Oct. 29 . . . . Prohibition plebiscite is creating quite a discussion. Rev. John Service of Kirk Church made himself either famous or notorious by preaching against the town council, the police force and my humble self. Accusations and retractions flying in all directions. We are living in a hot corner. God, I hope government control wins for this is one hell of a farce. — K.B.R.

Nov. 20 . . . . Had an earthquake shook [sic] night before last. Was sitting in the car at the time and felt her shake. Found today that bottles of rum standing in the cell had been tipped over. Shock followed by violent storms and high tide.

Had a great evening last Friday. All the bunch in the Camp started telling stories about hidden treasure and about ghosts.

Didnt get to sleep for two hours after I got home.

Got fine bonus of beer at the station today.

Yes Government control won the day by 25,000 majority so democracy is safe after all.

Dec. 14 . . . . Life is slipping along fairly smooth at present but the bumps will soon come thick and fast with the town elections.

Xmas 1929. Well it has come again and has almost gone. Old Santa has been very good to us all . . . .

I've had the best Xmas Ive ever had. Last night the bunch at my instigation consisting of Chief Caldwell, Officers Langille, Wright, Boone, Seaman, along with Councillors Milligan, Bannerman, and Grant and myself went to David Cullins restaurant at [?] and regaled ourselves until five in the morning. We had one grand time. Town wide open. The public diningroom was packed and going strong when I came home . . . .

Jan. 22, 1930 . . . . Had a stiff bye-election in Halifax yesterday. Dr. Murphy conservative elected by 5,400 majority. Sinclair, our magistrate wont be fit to go near for a month he is so pevish and petulant, he was the liberal leader.

Old James A. Fraser, Editor of the Eastern Chronicle died Wednesday at the ripe age of 89. He lived a full vigorous life his intellect keen right up to the end.

I'm not doing much to prosecute bootleggers now. I hope it wont be long until it's over . . . .

Feb. 8 . . . . The old timers are going fast this winter. Robt. Murray of McGregor and Company was buried yesterday . . . . George Grant elected Mayor by acclamation. Fred Milligan and he had a falling out. Some jealousy on Milligans part. Tom McKay hired young Oliver to fill a bottle of rum and hide it in Paddy Nolan's. Then Oliver telephoned him to come and get it. Traps and counter-traps. Intrigue, strategms and artifice . . . .

Feb. 10 . . . . Fred Milligan and George Grant still into it. Kind of childish.

Feb. 12 . . . . Was down to Egerton to see Uncle Bill Wilson. Poor old fellow I felt sorry for him. Done out of his farm and now dependent on a few dollars given him by his relatives to keep him out of the poorhouse. None of us can tell what our latter end will be.

Good hockey match last night between New Glasgow and Halifax. N.G. won.

Feb. 16 . . . . Are celebrating our 14 wedding anniversary by inviting McFadgns to tea . . . .

Well, went through a peculiar piece of underground manipulating last week. By an underground route learned of Chadwick, new Catholic liberal councillor framing an investigation of the police force prompted from Doug Gbrame's [Graham's] office. How to block it was the question. Here's where I subscribe to the ancient dictum. Its better to have three good friends than a million dollars without them. So I had to talk with H. McGrr, Catholic tory chairman of the ward. He went to Father ------- and at this period of writing the plot seems frustrated. Subterranean manipulation but it's a case where craft meets craft.

March 2 . . . . I see that the last entry was on Feb. 16 — a night of consequences. Langille and I planned and executed a perfect raid on Dolores Mc-------- in the middle of howling snowstorm in [?] Sunday. God, what a forsaken country. Roads were good to French River. Then took a sleigh to the lumber camp. Had the best cook I've ever found in a camp . . . .

March 9 . . . . Well Big Jack McLean was beaten in his election in Ward I last Tuesday — a bye election. This is the first election in which I have taken part for six years in which we were trimmed. I guess its the handwriting on the wall. Hon John Doull dont know his onions.

April 6 . . . . Hectic events in the small circle of our lives have happened. Under pressure of the Grant-Milligan fight we had to get Paddy Nolan. Result Milligan opens up, threatens dire results. By strategy I get the fine from Paddy Nolan before Milligan gets hold of him. Milligan goes up in the air, Paddy gets drunk assaults my buddy Sergeant Langille, is arrested and charged with assault. Milligan goes wild threatens Langille with his life. At the trial, Paddy is convicted of assault, appeals etc. But Milligan shoots his ammunition consequently is placed with his back to the wall. Swallows himself.

The chief, Langille and I are paraded before the bombastic Catholic liberal councillor, Chadwick but we hold our ground and in the words of the Eastern Chronicle Inspector Rose emerged winning the heats first money and cleaning up the purses.

As usual a great calm has followed the storm and the town is quiet.

This damd job has got my goat again. Milligan has come home from New York. Chadwick has designated Tom Bannerman as my "Boss" so I've written out my resignation and intend sending it in tomorrow.

May 24 . . . . Well since the last notation I have severed the cord that for over four years with various ebbs and flos has bound me to the rum wing of the body politic.

My resignation was a gem and a copy of it is worthy of implanting in this diary.

May 5th 1930

To his Worship the Mayor, etc.

I hereby tender my resignation as inspector for the Town of New Glasgow for the following reasons. Some three years ago following a vigorous prosecution of the N.S.T.A. my health was shattered and I cant see myself as being fool enough to make bad worse by making a thundering drive in the dying hours of the hunt.

Also, I decline to be made the football and goat of the whims and feuds of those in authority.

. . . . Am now a gentleman of leisure. But, there are a hell of a bunch in the Town Council now. And it was a grand finale that I gave them. Finished with colors flying . . . .

June 9 . . . . Have started in building fireplaces of the rustic nature. Built one for J.H. Millor and have one to build for Fred Milligan. Have lost the run of things around town.

Sept. 7. I find that I have been dallying in my work of keeping my diary all this livelong glorious summer, a summer surfeited with fine weather and life slipping by without the excitement so dramatically connected with the N.S.T.A. which went out of commission on August 18.

As I look over the last three months there are but few incidents worthy of recording. The launching of the "Morning Glory" a boat I built for Buddy. A trip I gave the children around the province, their interest in the thrifty Dutchman on the south shore, the building of a flower bed on the porch and my own fireplace so much for this book of four years well spent.

GLOSSARY OF NAMES

A.J. BANNERMAN was a lumberman and local politician of Liberal persuasion from Kenzieville.

JAMES CALDWELL, a senior police officer, became chief while Rose was with the force.

Col. THOMAS CANTLEY was Conservative M.P. for Pictou County.

CLIFFORD DANE, a labour organizer originally from Australia, was in 1920 president of the Nova Scotia Federation of Labour.

JOHN DOULL, brother-in-law of Alex McGregor, was mayor of New Glasgow in 1925 before winning election as M.L.A. for Pictou County.

J.C. DOUGLAS, a former mayor of Glace Bay veteran M.L.A., and one of the leading Conservatives in Cape Breton, resigned his post as provincial Attorney-General to contest Antigonish-Guysborough in the federal election of 1926.

SIR ANDREW RAE DUNCAN, a British lawyer with extensive industrial experience, investigated the labour-management problems of the coal industry as chairman of a provincial royal commission in 1925, and the problems and claims of the region as a whole as chairman of a federal royal commission in 1926.

JAMES A. FRASER was the ancient but peppery editor of the Liberal New Glasgow *Eastern Chronicle*. An anti-confederate in 1867, provincial M.L.A. and leading secessionist in the 1880's, Fraser was nominated by Pictou County Liberals in the federal election of 1926 as a symbol of regional protest. His skill at pungent invective was unequalled in the province.

J. STANLEY FRASER, a young defence lawyer often employed by those in the liquor trade, later became provincial organizer for the Conservatives in Nova Scotia.

R.D. GRAHAM was a prominent Liberal and defense lawyer often employed by those in the liquor trade.

Rev. D.K. GRANT was a lawyer and clergyman whom the newly-elected Conservative administration appointed chief temperance inspector for Nova Scotia.

GEORGE GRANT was a prominent New Glasgow businessman, councillor and mayor.

Rev. Dr. H.R. GRANT, a native Pictonian, was secretary of the provincial social service council and, from early in the century, the undisputed leader of the "dry" forces in Nova Scotia.

A.T. LOGAN was the chief of a corps of federal preventative officers in the province.

E.M. MACDONALD was a veteran Liberal M.P. for Pictou County and cabinet minister, who in 1925 won election in Antigonish-Guysborough.

ALEX MACGREGOR, a former M.P., was the reputed political boss and master-strategist for the Conservatives in Pictou County.

ROD G. MACKAY was the prosecuting lawyer against the liquor trade in New Glasgow.

TOM MACKAY was a former New Glasgow temperance inspector who became deputy-provincial inspector for eastern Nova Scotia.

DANNIE MACLENNAN was reputed to be the leading liquor retailer in New Glasgow.

AMY MASON, "Queen of the Smugglers" and a native Pictonian, was one of the major distributors of liquor in the province.

FRED MILLIGAN was a local Conservative politician, New Glasgow town councillor and businessman. His feud with Walter Weir disrupted party organization in the county particularly as related to the liquor trade.

PADDY NOLAN, ex-hockey player of note and Conservative protégé of Fred Milligan was permitted for a time to sell liquor in New Glasgow unmolested.

E.N. RHODES, an Ontario businessman formerly of Amherst, returned to Nova Scotia shortly before the election of 1925, secured the leadership of the provincial Conservative party, and led it to victory on a platform which featured a campaign for Maritime Rights.

BUDDIE was Clifford Rose's young son.

D.C. SINCLAIR was a New Glasgow magistrate of Liberal background.

WALTER WEIR was a local Conservative politician, ex-councillor and business associate of Tom MacKay.

Date Due